A well-researched, comprehensive roadmap to freedom, this book is a must-read for anyone seeking the way out of an abusive relationship. I wish it had been available when I needed it. It is spot on.

—Rose Booth, abuse survivor and strong, independent woman.

A thorough, comprehensive, and inclusive book for the women of the world. It will be immensely helpful to those who have been abused and neglected or have ever felt like a victim. What a gift!

—Cath DePalma, author I *Can Do This Thing Called Life: And So Can You!* and *Energize Your Creative Super Powers: 7 Ways to Spiritual Fitness.*

Well thought out and well researched. A straightforward sharing of experience and advice that will both touch readers and move them to action. The author's honest and heartfelt intentions come through clearly.

—Dawn Murphy, author *Physical Stuff & Mental Junk: A Minimalist Path to True Abundance* and *Separate No More: Inviting Peace, Embracing Diversity & Creating a Positive Future.*

A fantastic book. Transforming. I couldn't stop reading. The vast majority of my clients are abused women. I will recommend this book to all of them!

—Kathleen L. Quinlan, LMT, Transformational Heart and Soul Healing.

Filled with helpful resources, *No More Abuse* provides insight and practical advice from a woman who faced domestic abuse and stared it down. I wish this book had been available when I was counseling parishioners and clients suffering from abuse.

—Rev. Allen E. Schenk (ret.), M.Div., STM, Clinical Fellow AAPC, Clinical Diplomat APA.

No More Abuse

From the hard-earned wisdom of a survivor . . .

No More Abuse

How To Leave Your Abuser, Reconnect with Yourself & Create a New Life

by T. Ann DeCarlo

WingSpan Press

Published in the United States and the United Kingdom by WingSpan Press, Livermore, CA

The WingSpan name, logo, and colophon are the trademarks of WingSpan Publishing.

ISBN 978-1-63683-037-7 (pbk.)
ISBN 978-1-63683-970-7 (ebk.)

Printed in the United States of America

www.wingspanpress.com

Edited by Susan Owens
Tales for Telling, LLC, Lexington, Kentucky

Publisher's Cataloging-in-Publication Data

Names: DeCarlo, T. Ann. 1955- .
Title: No more abuse : how to leave your abuser, reconnect with yourself & create a new life / T. Ann DeCarlo.
Description: Livermore, CA : WingSpan Press, 2023. |
Identifiers: LCCN 2022923109 | ISBN 9781636830377 (pbk.) | ISBN 9781636839707 (ebook)
Subjects: LCSH: Family violence. | Marital violence. | Spousal abuse. | BISAC: SELF-HELP / Abuse. | SELF-HELP / Safety & Security / General. | SELF-HELP / Self-Management / General.
Classification: LCC HV6626.D43 2023 | DDC 362.8292 D--dc23
LC record available at https://lccn.loc.gov/2022923109

To every woman who is now living with an abuser,

And to every woman who has had or will have the courage to leave.

Disclaimer

The material in this book is intended to help women identify abusive and potentially abusive relationships, safely remove themselves from their abusers, and move on to a new life. It is not intended as a substitute for the advice of a trained counselor, therapist, or other mental health professional. If you are currently in counseling or therapy, check with your mental health provider before altering or discontinuing your therapeutic regimen.

While the author has made every effort to provide dependable information, accurate telephone numbers, and valid Internet addresses, neither the publisher, the author, nor the editor assumes any responsibility for changes that occur after publication.

The contents of the book have been compiled through research and personal experience. However, the reader should be aware that professionals in the field have differing opinions. Therefore the author and editor, as well as the professionals quoted in this book, cannot be held responsible for any error, omission, professional disagreement, or dated material. The author assumes no responsibility for any outcome of applying the information in this book in a program of self-care or under the care of a licensed practitioner. If you have questions about the application of the information described herein, consult a licensed therapist.

If you are in a violent or potentially violent relationship, please call the domestic abuse hotline: National Domestic Violence HOTLINE, 1-800-799-SAFE (7233). If you are in immediate danger, call 911.

The Journey

—Mary Oliver

One day you finally knew
what you had to do, and began,
though the voices around you
kept shouting
their bad advice—
though the whole house began to tremble
and you felt the old tug at your ankles.
"Mend my life!" each voice cried,
But you didn't stop.
You knew what you had to do,
though the wind pried
with its stiff fingers
at the very foundations,
though their melancholy was terrible.
It was already late enough,
and a wild night,
and the road full of fallen
branches and stones.
But little by little,
as you left their voices behind,
the stars began to burn
through the sheets of clouds,
and there was a new voice which you slowly
recognized as your own, that kept you company
as you strode deeper and deeper into the world,
determined to do the only thing you could do,
determined to save the only life you could save.[1]

Contents

Section Two

Section Three

Acknowledgments

So many people helped create this book. Without them, it would still be a nagging idea in my brain.

To my editor and sister, Susan Owens, whose grasp of the English language and talent with the written word have forged a perfect merger in her career as a personal historian. Our grandmother was a writer. Both she and our mother taught English, and their talents live on through Susan. I'm in awe of your ability to see the statue in the rock of the draft I created. I can never thank you enough.

To Edward Zelinsky, whose artistic talent provided the perfect cover design and whose belief in this project provided just the support I needed, just when I needed it.

To my dear friends Keri Darlington, Cath DePalma, Kathleen Quinlan, Brenda Lancaster, Dawn Murphy, and Al Schenk, who provided support and/or review. Your encouragement, sharing of personal experiences, and professional opinions enhanced my words and kept me going. All of you light up my life.

To the professionals and organizations who gave me permission to use their words. Your writing helped me understand my past; your generosity will help my readers find their way to freedom. Thank you for your encouragement and expertise.

American Academy of Experts in Traumatic Stress
Tina de Benedictis, PhD; Jaelline Jaffe, PhD; Jeanne Segal, PhD
Donna Ashworth
Brené Brown, PhD
Sandra L. Brown, MA
Thomas G. Fiffer, MA
Susan Forward, PhD
Harville Hendrix, PhD, and Helen LaKelly Hunt, PhD
National Domestic Violence Hotline
Robin Norwood
Grove Atlantic (Mary Oliver poem "The Journey")
Leon Seltzer, PhD
George Simon, PhD
Shannon Thomas, LCSW
John B. Waterhouse, PhD

Introduction

"A journey of a thousand miles begins with a single step."
—Chinese Proverb

I didn't care if I lived or died the night I escaped. Numbed by years of emotional, verbal, and threatened physical abuse, I was beyond sadness, or anger, or even fear. I felt absolutely nothing.

As I look back on that night, I realize how lucky I was. My lack of emotion enabled me to think clearly enough to get out of the house unharmed. I remained calm while he came apart. I knew the gun in the drawer next to him was loaded, but it didn't matter. He couldn't hurt me anymore; inside I was dead already.

I drove around the corner and rolled down the window, waiting calmly for the sound of a gunshot. Since he hadn't used the gun on me, I thought it quite possible he would use it on himself. When after a few minutes no sound pierced the still night air, I stopped considering whether I'd call 911 and drove to a friend's house. Fortunately, my husband didn't know where I was going, nor did he know where my friend lived. She and I would be safe for the night.

Like that of many abusers, his jealousy of anyone in my life—friends, family, co-workers, clients—resulted in my isolation. It's common for abuse victims to succumb to the brainwashing tactics that slowly but surely erode their self-esteem. I was no exception. Like countless others before me, I began to keep my situation to myself, feeling embarrassed or perhaps deserving of the cruel treatment I received. After all, he wasn't hitting me (just breaking things around me and threatening to beat me into submission) and, like many victims, I didn't realize the definition and insidious nature of emotional and verbal abuse. Back then, this type of non-physical abuse simply didn't have a label, or at least not a label I was aware of. It wasn't a topic I'd ever seen discussed in magazines or on TV, and the World Wide Web did not yet exist.

I was isolated and didn't understand the severity of my situation. I didn't know there were organizations that could help me get out safely. I didn't have a plan to leave under safe conditions. I hadn't confided in a friend or family member who might have helped. I escaped despite all of these barriers, but I was very, very lucky. The outcome could have been far worse.

I believe with all my heart that if I would have known then what I know now, I would have, at best, walked away from my future husband long before we married. At the very least, I would have left my marriage years before I did.

My abusive marriage ended more than three decades ago, but it was many years before I completely understood the forces that attracted me to him in the first place and kept me with him for so long.

I've written this book to give you the tools and knowledge I didn't have when I needed them. This information is drawn from my years of experience as an abused spouse, what I learned from therapy, my journey through personal growth and various methods of healing, and interviews/writings of numerous trained experts on this subject. Within these pages:

- You'll discover how to recognize the red flags of a potential abuser before you're sucked into a hellish relationship.

- You'll learn how abuse escalates and manifests itself in many ways other than physical assault; why you are not the cause of his actions; why no woman will ever be able to please him;

why no woman has the magic bullet to make an abuser stop; why it is nearly impossible for him to change; and the mental illness that is behind it all.

- You'll find words of encouragement, strength, and support for your decision to take back your power and your life, plus access to counsel and assistance on how to do so safely.

- You'll learn about services provided by the many shelters that exist solely to support you, from helping you make a safe escape plan to assisting with relocation, housing, divorce, job and financial training, and healing. Many shelters also offer facilities to house your animals. The goal of these organizations is to provide the resources that will let you and your children begin an independent and safe life. Services vary depending on the shelter, but all services are free. (See *Chapter 8 – Services Provided by Local Shelters* for a more detailed list of services that may be offered in your area.)

- You'll also find guidance for healing and moving forward once you have escaped. This process entails regaining your mental freedom, courage, and strength, as well as learning how to avoid duplicating past choices. Untethering yourself from the past eliminates its power over you. Uncovering your dreams and unearthing who you are can help you to trust and love yourself again (or perhaps for the first time) and sets you free to live a full and wonderful life.

- You'll receive further help with future decisions through learning about the characteristics of a good man and the features of a healthy relationship. When and if you decide you're ready to date again, you'll have the tools you need to choose a mentally stable and emotionally supportive long-term partner. You'll also learn to recognize the red flags in today's dating world, as well as how to do an Internet background check on a potential partner.

No More Abuse

No one deserves abuse, physical or emotional. No one! No matter what you may have been told by your abuser or others, there are no exceptions to this rule. It is my fondest hope that the information that follows will give you the strength, courage, and knowledge you need to safely begin a new life of freedom and joy.

Section One

*T*his portion of the book is written for those of you who think you might be involved with an abuser and for those of you who know you are. It contains the eye-opening knowledge you need right now in order to evaluate the reality of your situation.

I know, beyond a doubt, that if I had been privy to the information explained in these first eight chapters, I would have been spared many years of misery.

My greatest hope is that something you read in these pages helps you begin your path to freedom and a life of safety, support, kindness, laughter, and most of all, love.

Chapter 1

Recognizing Early-Warning Red Flags

"How do you end up with a prince? By not settling for a frog!"
—T. Ann DeCarlo

I remember sitting in a restaurant, across the table from the man who would become my husband. Back then we were still college kids and he was describing his childhood, calmly telling me about the day he'd raised a shotgun and pulled the trigger after finding his father, yet again, standing over his mother's beaten body. Fortunately or unfortunately, depending on how you look at it, the gun was not loaded. A family life of control and physical abuse was all he'd ever known.

Could the red flags have been any more obvious? They were neon and massive and waving frantically but, lacking any education on the subject of abuse, I couldn't see them. The whole concept was completely foreign to me.

So what *was* going through my young brain? Probably something along the lines of, *Oh, this poor man. He hated his home life, but he got out, got an education, and would never treat his wife the way his father treated his mother. Look how well he treats me! I know he thinks I'm special; after all, he confided in me. And I can make it all better.*

There are times when ignorance is definitely not bliss.

If we had a crystal ball that could tell us, with total certainty, that the person showing interest in us, or who is interesting *to* us, was or would become abusive, it would certainly make life easier and safer. Unfortunately, such a magic orb exists only in fairy tales.

What we do have is access to education. Education that gives us the ability to recognize red flags. Education that teaches us to pay attention to that uneasy feeling in our gut and the little voice in our head before we entwine ourselves in another person's life. Gaining faith in our own intuition and ability to avoid unacceptable individuals goes a long way toward keeping us safe.

The bottom line is this: The earlier you recognize the signs of an abusive man, the easier it is to walk away. Fortunately, most abusers put out one or more warning signs early in the relationship.

In this age of social media and digital recordkeeping, it's also possible to discover a huge amount about a potential partner via Internet background-checking sites such as BeenVerified, Truthfinder, InstantCheckMate, and PeopleLooker.

Unfortunately, such sites cannot access public court records such as divorce proceedings or domestic-violence injunctions (sometimes called restraining orders or protective orders).[2] Some states may make such orders more difficult to access as an added level of protection for the petitioner. To confirm whether someone is divorced or has been charged with domestic violence, you'll need to know his full name and the state and county in which the papers were filed. The address history provided by the background-checking sites may allow you to determine the county or counties you'll need to access. Begin by Googling *how to find divorce records* in the appropriate state. Armed with this information, go online to the appropriate state or county court site and search for divorce and/or injunction filings. If the state/county does not offer Internet access to these records, use the information from your Google search to call the county clerk of the court or the relevant state-level department to learn how you can access this information. (For more on how to do an Internet background check, see *Chapter 20 – How to Investigate a Potential Partner*.)

Getting Out *Before* Getting Involved

At this early stage of the dating game, you are voluntarily interacting with a man and observing his behavior. If he begins to display the warning signs of abusive conduct and you ignore or try to rationalize them, your status begins to morph from volunteer to victim. The more deeply you become involved with an intimidating man, the stronger the cage he builds around you and the more difficult it becomes to escape.

Take it slow; proceed with caution: I'm surprised at how television and movies foster a total lack of caution when it comes to relationships. Two people meet and the next scene takes place in the bedroom. The potentially life-threatening consequences of this throw-caution-to-the-wind behavior are left off the table. The couple spends no time getting to know one another and never seem to worry about, let alone discuss, sexually transmitted diseases (STDs).[3]

Even if you are interested only in casual sex, the intimacy could trigger a whole set of control issues in your partner. Next thing you know you're dealing with a stalker who's constantly texting, showing up at your home or place of business unannounced, or worse.

In other words, for safety's sake take the time to get to know the person before you hop into bed. Meet in public places and talk for a period of time. Initially, keep information like where you live and the location of your work to yourself. Abusers are like the proverbial wolf in sheep's clothing: They are adept at appearing to be the exact opposite of their true selves. Give your awareness and intuition a chance to keep you safe before you allow someone into your life.

It is also imperative to discover if you are compatible with a potential partner in areas beyond physical attraction. In his book

Will Our Love Last? Sam R. Hamburg, PhD, provides practical, easy-to-understand guidance on how to determine compatibility and why it is essential for long-term, healthy relationships. *In my opinion, everyone entering the dating arena should read this book.*

Slowing things down makes it easier to assess your degree of compatibility with a potential partner, to see what kind of guy he is at a day-to-day level, and to gain a much clearer view of his real personality. Not only will you be able to make better decisions about how and whether you want to get closer, you'll also have the opportunity to build a connection based on what's *really* there, rather than on some romantic ideal of what you wish were so. No matter what pressures you may feel from society or the other person to move quickly, it's vital you do what is best for you. *You are running the show!*

In far too many instances, modern society equates sexual intimacy with real intimacy. In actuality, sexual intimacy embraced too soon in a relationship thwarts the process of getting to know a potential partner. Because sex speeds up the intensity of emotional involvement, opportunities to develop the core building blocks of openness, trust, and honesty—the traits of a truly solid connection—are often missed. Whirlwind courtships foster a pseudo-intimacy often mistaken for genuine closeness. And a lot of guys can be very good at separating sex from emotion, so you can't assume that sleeping with a guy will bring you closer to him.

Sex is not a substitute form of communication. Without a strong foundation based on trust, friendship, and mutual respect—the basis of true intimacy—sex becomes a couple's default language. But sex does not build that strong foundation; it only muddies the waters.

I realize taking it slow isn't in sync with today's warp-speed, "you should end up in the sack by the third date" standards. However, if sex is involved, even the most inappropriate partner can be seen to do no wrong. Once the love drug takes over, the corresponding biological emotional currents greatly impair the ability to assess a partner realistically. The love drug takes over even if sex is not yet involved. A focused interest in the other person is enough to set it free.

Beware of the love drug (PEA): Have you ever wondered why we feel so exhilarated just thinking about a new potential partner? During the initial stage of romantic "love," it's normal to find it hard to think or talk about anything other than the object of our affection. Nothing else matters. Our jobs, families, friends, and personal interests are steamrollered by an overpowering desire to be with our new love. We feel as though we're floating on a cloud…like we're drugged.

In reality, we *are* drugged. Budding romance is enhanced by the brain's production of a natural amphetamine (mood elevator and antidepressant) called phenylethylamine (PEA), also known as the love drug. The role of PEA is to bring two people together to start the bonding process. According to Harville Hendrix, PhD, co-founder of Imago Relationship Therapy with his wife, Helen LaKelly Hunt, PhD, PEA enables us to attach to a partner without seeing any of his or her negative characteristics until the drug starts to fade. Very roughly, PEA production is estimated to last about three months past the point of some level of commitment.

When PEA is raging through our system, love really *is* blind. Our love interest can do no wrong. Once the drug wears off, assuming we still like what we see, a good relationship should soften into feelings of safety, contentment, and balance. If not, something is wrong.

As I learned the hard way and confirmed through reading the works of various professionals (see *Chapter 21 – Resources and*

References), it's common for abusive men to be extremely talented at making their partners feel special during courtship. They show an intense level of caring, along with respect and adoration. The thing is, they can't sustain the charade for long. Their true colors will normally be exposed after a few short months.

For example, let's say the first clue about a potential partner's true nature takes the form of verbal denigration, such as screaming at you in public and/or calling you various names. When under the influence of PEA, you will be more inclined to rationalize his bad behavior… *he's tired, he's had a bad day,* etc. It is so easy to sweep red flags under the rug when this new, amazing person makes you feel so good. In reality, he's testing you. Will you take it or will you let him know in no uncertain terms that he's totally out of line and you're not going to stay with anyone who treats you that way? No matter which option you choose, you're teaching him how to treat you. Abuse begins with a series of boundary violations left unaddressed. Abusers abuse because they can; their partners unwittingly, slowly allow them to get away with it.

I experienced this particular red flag a few years ago. I was intensely and loudly criticized by a man I had dated for a very short time when we were inside a store. By the time the incident occurred, however, I was well aware of the meaning behind this controlling behavior. It was the first time he had shown his true colors and the last time I saw him.

According to Sandra L. Brown, MA, author of *How to Spot a Dangerous Man Before You Get Involved,* the abusive man interprets silence and staying with him as acceptance of his behavior. She explains it this way: Even if you voice concerns about what he just did to you, he has learned you'll take what he dishes out *because you stay.*

The point is, no one has the right to treat you in an abusive manner, and it's important to shut him down and *walk away immediately*. Ask yourself if you ever would do to another person what he just did to you. A kind and good man does not blow up like that, especially in public. Don't buy his apologies. Rationalization of bad behavior always leads to a miserable relationship.

Obviously, it's better to wait out the romantic "high," giving yourself the opportunity to truly evaluate the other person before making any long-term commitments. Devoid of PEA, you can determine if this person is worthy of you, is committed to you, respects you, encourages you to grow, has your best interests at heart, and enhances rather than constricts your life.

Ignoring society's pressures to pursue a relationship at breakneck speed, taking the time to get to know your potential partner, understanding the rose-colored-glasses effect of the "love drug," and recognizing the early-warning signs outlined in this chapter will help you walk away before you're trapped.

My Experience with PEA

By the time I removed myself from my soulless marriage, I thought my body was dead. I'd had no interest in sex or making love—yes, these are definitely two different things—for years. My libido had atrophied from boredom, disgust, and fear. The idea of letting a man touch me caused revulsion and nausea.

After a year and a half of post-marriage, deep internal travel designed to unearth and release old detrimental beliefs, I felt ready to stick my toe into the dating pool. The man who caught my eye leaned toward spirituality, and he made it quite clear from our first phone conversation that taking time to get to know one another was imperative. He was also interested in engaging in

13

good conversation, a new experience for both of us. Okay, I was hooked. What I didn't see coming was how I found this type of open communication explosively attractive. I also found many other things about him to be attractive, both inside and out.

Then it happened: I was bombarded by PEA. It was like becoming incredibly turned on during an intimate encounter but finding that state of arousal to be permanent. My body was alive again and on fire, something I sincerely didn't think could happen. True, I was seeing behavior in him that didn't thrill me, but I didn't care. Although it was way too soon for a sexual relationship, I simply craved the affection, attention, and connection between us. I thought he was a good man. It turned out I was wrong, but after so many years, it was wonderful to believe he found me attractive and intelligent and to experience the normal give and take of two-way communication, devoid of criticism and judgment. These feelings took priority over everything and anything else. By this time I'd read and studied enough to know exactly what was happening, and why. Having this knowledge, however, provided not even the tiniest thread of control over what was going on in my brain. I was completely blindsided by PEA.

After dating him for just seven weeks, I came down with a doozy of a cold and couldn't see him, or anyone else, for eleven days. During this time the PEA started to dissipate, my hormones shrank and fell through the sieve, and I was left with a pile of reality. Once I saw the relationship without my rose-colored glasses (about the tenth day of my illness), I was appalled at how much I'd invested in a man I realized I didn't even like. I ended it then and there.

I gained an entirely new respect for the power of PEA through this experience, as well as the benefits of taking things slowly in a new relationship. I hope my experience offers the same insight to you.

Early-Warning Red Flags

Some women don't believe they are in abusive relationships because their partners are not hitting them (yet). I was one of these women. Abuse takes many forms beyond physical. Although often unseen and unacknowledged, abuse of other kinds—verbal, emotional, spiritual, financial, or sexual—leaves women with scars just as deep and just as painful as the scars of physical violence.

The paragraphs below provide examples of red flags for all forms of abuse. All may not apply to every abuser, and having one or more of them does not mean that a man is necessarily an abuser. (For example, not every single man who comes from an abusive background becomes an abuser as an adult.) However, when you encounter these red flags it's important to treat them like flashing road signs: "Warning: Dangerous Conditions Ahead," and end the relationship.

He had an abusive upbringing: A strong predictor of domestic violence in adulthood is domestic violence in the household in which a person was reared. The cycle of domestic violence is difficult to break because parents have presented violence as a normal relationship skill.

Listen closely to his stories when the subject of his home life comes up. Is he a product of an abusive household? If he is a product of abuse and control, did he become aware of his inherent lack of relationship skills at some point in time? What method(s) did he use to overcome his upbringing?

One of the therapists I interviewed for this book explained that if a man has gone to therapy and has made a total about-face in his life, he is generally very willing, even eager, to talk about it.

If your potential partner has not received help, pay attention to the red flags. Even if he says how much he hated his father for what he did, he can easily repeat the same behavior due to his ignorance of healthy relationship skills. I've experienced this scenario firsthand.

He is disrespectful of previous partners: I'm sure the subject of marriage or previous long-term relationships will be part of your discussions, assuming either of you has been down that road a time or two. Determining how a potential partner dealt with previous partners is doubly important if he was raised in an abusive household. Does he recognize his part in the demise of the union or does he place all the blame on his previous partner(s)? Does he seem focused on denigrating his ex-spouse(s)? Does he mention pursuing any type of therapy during the relationship or after it ended?

People without abusive tendencies are more likely to learn from a failed relationship and acknowledge their degree of participation in its failure. Abusers, on the other hand, find their behavior absolutely justified and see no reason to change. They were just trying to make their partner "a better person."

The red flags are waving frantically when you perceive a lack of introspection, no acknowledgment of mistakes, the inability to accept any portion of the responsibility for the failure of a relationship, and/or the recurring theme that everyone else is to blame.

Eventually, the disrespect he voiced toward previous partners could be directed at you.

He believes women are generally selfish: Because an abusive man will only be happy with a woman who exists solely for the purpose of serving him at the expense of a life of her own, he has obviously not been able to engage in a happy long-term relationship. As a result, abusers generally lump women together in a category labeled "selfish and greedy."

Of course, you are the exception. You are "special and different" from anyone he's ever met. It's normal to feel this way about a new person in your life, but look beyond the wonderful feeling this gives you to see if any red flags are flying. If he labels women as generally inadequate and acknowledges no role in the failure of any previous relationships, bolt for the door.

He wants to get serious quickly: It's easy to be flattered by someone who is extremely interested in you and/or wants a committed relationship ASAP. If he's asking for exclusivity or another form of commitment way too soon, raise your red-flag antenna. In reality, you could be witnessing panic and the first step to trap you.

The abuser wants ownership of his partner, and the thought of a new potential partner seeing someone else and having a life of her own dredges up his main fear: abandonment. This is why his goal is to lock you into a committed relationship before you have time to change your mind.

I know that for many of us it is hard to hurt someone's feelings or to walk away from a man who is offering attention. We are hardwired to want companionship, but companionship should not come *at the expense of losing yourself.* Honor yourself by not allowing this type of insecure man into your life.

He pressures you for sex: If a man is attempting to pressure you into an intimate relationship using guilt, promises of love, threats to break off the relationship, or any other buttons he chooses to push, this behavior is a huge red flag. He isn't hearing you or honoring your wishes. His motives are strictly selfish. You are witnessing exploitation and a form of sexual abuse. Abusers see women as slaves with whom they have vaginal rights rather than as human beings. Eventually, you won't have much say in the matter. Run for the hills.

He has a sketchy employment record: Has he had multiple jobs, been laid off and/or fired several times, or experienced multiple business failures? Does he place 100 percent of the blame on circumstances "beyond his control" and/or on the other people involved? Don't be tempted to rush in and provide economic aid for this person. A man with this background could take serious financial advantage of you via consistent excuses and blame-ridden unemployment.

He thinks everyone else is to blame: If you see a consistent pattern of blaming everyone else for things that have gone wrong in his life and not being able to accept or acknowledge his contribution to why things went wrong, be assured you will ultimately be the target of his blame.

He justifies his control based on religion: Some men hide behind religion as justification for control and abuse of a partner. The most common religious scriptures can be misinterpreted to support male domination and female submission.

An abusive man also may feel quite justified in controlling the spiritual beliefs of his partner. Does he internalize a strong belief in one religious tradition and find it very important that you believe the same? Is he a religious fanatic with beliefs in female submission? If so, be aware of his potential for abuse.

Holding strong, aggressive feelings of prejudice toward people of other races, ethnicities, or religions is another red flag.

He has financially controlling ideas: Is he convinced that women should not have a career or that a man's career is more important than a woman's? Would he be intimidated if his partner's income exceeded his? Does he believe that the man should have total control of the money? Is he intimidated by a woman maintaining any degree of financial independence such as separate credit cards or checking/savings accounts?

Total financial control is one of the main ways abusers entrap their partners. Escape is very difficult without access to money.

He exhibits inappropriate anger and aggression: Everybody gets ticked off once in a while, but an abusive man is intimidating and frightening when he gets angry. Be on the lookout for mood swings and an explosive temper. When angered he may drive recklessly, punch walls, push you, throw things, or tower over you.

It has been my experience that anger and control go hand in hand. Involvement with an angry person can be difficult at best and life-threatening at worst. Once you accept a verbal attack, the transition from volunteer to victim has begun. Do not pass Go; do not collect $200. Head for the door and don't look back.

He shows early signs of control: Control begins in subtle ways as he slowly infringes on your boundaries. Perhaps he starts to "innocently" suggest you would look better if you changed your hairstyle, hair color, or wardrobe. Left to his own devices, he will feed his need for control by infesting all areas of your life.

No one has the right to tell you what to say, how to dress, where to work or not work, what to watch on TV, how to wear your hair, when to see your friends or family, what to read… The list goes on and on. (For a list of your basic human relationship rights, see *Chapter 19*.)

He's into possessiveness, jealousy, and isolation: Look for inclinations toward jealousy and insecurity during your get-to-know-one-another period. People with control issues are commonly threatened by the other people in their partner's or potential partner's lives. Their jealousies extend to both friends and family. It can begin with requests that you cancel your plans to attend events or spend time with family or friends because he misses you and wants to spend time with you. Finding fault with your friends or family may be the next isolation method he employs. *Big…. Red…. Flag….*

Our age of electronic gadgets offers multiple new ways for a person with control issues to act on their fears. Frequent texting, calling, or emailing, wanting to know where you are, is a definite red flag. This is not cute or a sign that he cares. *This Is Control!*

No partner has the right to look through your phone or other electronic devices without your permission. A man who crosses this boundary is exhibiting possessiveness, insecurity, control, jealousy, and, most of all, fear of what happens when you're not with him. He must isolate you in order to subdue this fear. Never leave your phone unattended while you're getting to know someone.

Know that you do not ever need to alter what you want to do or where you want to go or who you are in order to pacify another person's insecurities. Insecurity can only be addressed by the individual who has it. He must be willing to recognize the issue, have the desire to fix it, and demonstrate the dedication to secure professional help for however long is necessary. Insecurity is not characteristic of a good life partner.

Is your life an open book exposed on social networks? Unfortunately, this medium can make it easier for anyone to keep track of you. If you begin to receive out-of-context questions about other people in your photos or about who you were with when you attended some event you posted on social media, raise your red-flag antenna.

Do these questions seem normal to you based on previous conversations, or do they border on creepy? For example, normal might be: "I saw the last photos you posted. Was that the relative you told me about who lives in Milwaukee?" On the other hand, "Why didn't you tell me you were going out? Who were those people? Where did you go after the event?

Who was that other guy? How do you know him? What does he mean to you? What time did you get home?" is definitely creepy!

Whatever you do, don't let him talk you into adding a "find me" app to your phone. Thanks to this app, as long as your phone is turned on and you have it with you, he'll be able to track your every move. Even more disturbing are spyware apps: programs that allow him to track your every move and can be added to your phone without your knowledge. Apps such as Anti Spy can help you detect whether spyware is operating on your phone.

He has a problem with substance abuse: Not all abusers abuse drugs or alcohol, but because many kinds of abuse often go hand-in-hand, substance abuse is also a red flag. The likelihood of emotional abuse escalating to physical abuse increases when the abuser also abuses alcohol or drugs.

I've had friends who dated guys for many weeks before finding out these potential partners had issues with substance abuse—another reason to take your time getting to know someone before entering into an intimate relationship. So much can be hidden from view at first.

He has a problem with deception: Catching him in lies is another giant warning sign. For example, after giving you details and dates of his divorce, he eventually confesses that his divorce is actually just "in the works." By overlooking this blatant lie, you are letting him know he can step on you and you'll take it. It's also a sign that he will lie throughout your relationship whenever it benefits him. Trust is the foundation of marriage. If he can't be trusted, he can't be a good partner to anyone. Toss him to the curb.

He is self-absorbed and/or egotistical: Is he a good talker but a terrible listener? Does he continually switch the conversation

21

back to himself? Does he show little curiosity about who you are? This characteristic can be the tip of the iceberg if you're dealing with an abuser. As the relationship continues, the self-centeredness you originally detected will turn into a dictatorship as he expects your complete servitude.

He mistreats animals: Observe how he treats his pets. Can he relate to their needs? Does he do things like leaving his dogs outside without any shelter all year round, regardless of conditions or temperature, because he is unable to relate to their discomfort? If so, it's time to exit the building and for the sake of his animals, report him to the proper authorities.

He is a deadbeat dad: A man who can father a child and simply walk away from his responsibilities—financially, emotionally, or both—should generate a huge early-warning sign. Not all deadbeat dads are abusers, but their actions can be indicative of a lack of connection and empathy.

A good man would not exhibit any of the characteristics and behaviors indicated in this chapter.

Because the early-warning signs of abuse are often sporadic in the beginning stages of a relationship, taking things slowly gives you a chance to determine the true nature of the other person and, if necessary, remove yourself from the relationship before you become another one of his victims.

Chapter 2

From Person to Possession

"In whom there is no sympathy for living beings: know him as an outcast."
—the Buddha

*L*ittle do we know that when this seemingly charming, cute, smart, and funny man starts to show his true colors, we will be facing a common pattern of escalating domestic abuse shared by one in three women.

In my case, most of our courtship was long-distance. Seeing one another sporadically allowed him to keep his true nature hidden. I knew his background was fraught with control and physical abuse, but his proclivity for this same behavior did not show up until after we tied the knot. Only then did he take off the mask. Up to that point, he had treated me with respect, admiration, and love.

I was broadsided by the immediate change in his demeanor, which began shortly after our wedding. On the first day we moved into our apartment, he told me I was *never* to question him. He even told me how to put dishes in the dishwasher. These and many other pronouncements were not to be taken as suggestions but as commands. Whatever he decided was law. He began listening to my phone conversations with family and instructed me as to what I could and could not say. The list of rules and criticisms seemed endless.

I began to question my own sanity. Was I imagining this change in his personality? Had it been there all along and I didn't see it?

No, I wasn't imagining it. The abuse in his background was one of many red flags that had been looming large all along, but I simply hadn't had enough experience to recognize it for what it was. I hadn't yet learned that an abrupt change from charming to control once a couple makes a commitment is not unusual for an abuser. All I knew was that I was terribly confused. Maybe, I figured, we were just experiencing the ups and downs sometimes characteristic of newly married couples and that in time everything would be fine.

It hurts when the person who made you feel so special yesterday makes you feel unwanted and unimportant today. Little did I know I had been conned into falling in love with the mask he wore while we were dating. He put on this same mask before he went out into the world each day, but he took it off as soon as he walked through our door. If I'd only known.

I had no family in the area and kept much of what I was going through to myself. It wasn't until several years later, after my mother sent me the book *Men Who Hate Women and the Women Who Love Them* by Dr. Susan Forward, that I knew I hadn't imagined my husband's instant Dr. Jekyll/Mr. Hyde personality change. I felt as though the author must have had hidden cameras in our first apartment and subsequent homes, because she somehow knew exactly what I was going through. It seemed as if she had written the book specifically for me.

I will be forever grateful to my mom for recognizing how much I needed that book. Not only did I learn about various events that can trigger the instant personality change of an abusive man, I also became aware that abuse escalates. Controlling behavior expands into verbal and emotional abuse and advanced methods of isolating one's partner. Breaking things around the "loved" one, along with the threat of physical abuse (implied or spoken), may occur before he crosses the line into physical abuse.

To an abuser, an intimate relationship is all about power and control. The women he abuses become imprisoned by manipulation and domination to such a degree they can become convinced they deserve such cruel treatment.

Abusers achieve their goals through a variety of methods, all of which are intertwined with emotional and verbal abuse:[4]

- Criticizing you

- Displaying temper tantrums/out-of-control anger

- Bouncing between love and hate

- Isolating you

- Eliminating your basic human rights

- Exhibiting jealousy and accusing you of having affairs

- Abandoning you emotionally

- Minimizing, denying, blaming

- Impoverishing you

- Causing physical harm

The remainder of this chapter reveals how these methods manifest themselves and escalate within an abusive relationship.

I didn't know it at the time, but Dr. Forward's book would be instrumental in helping me escape my marriage. Perhaps her words saved my life.

The longer you stay in an abusive relationship, the harder and more dangerous escape becomes. In past generations, many women had nowhere to turn. Today, at least in the United States, an amazing network is available to help you. All you have to do is reach out. Use a friend's phone or another safe phone (one your partner does not have access to) to dial the National Domestic Violence

HOTLINE, 1-800-799-SAFE (7233), and find out what types of help and support are available in your area. (Also see *Chapter 8 – Services Provided by Local Shelters* and *Chapter 21 – Resources and References.*) *You are not alone!*

It Will Only Get Worse: How Abuse Escalates

Constantly criticizing: His little "suggestions" as to your dress or hair or friends, etc., begin to morph into orders, unreasonable expectations, and subsequent belittling. He is the judge of what is right and what is wrong with you. Your opinion and judgment are worthless in his eyes. He sees nothing amiss with pointing out all of your "faults," explaining his behavior as "doing you a favor."

He may call you stupid, inconsiderate, ugly, and/or fat with the goal of eventually convincing you that no one else would ever love you. Sadly, it is normal for abused women to become so beaten down and brainwashed that they begin to define themselves by these labels.

Displaying temper tantrums and unpredictable, out-of-control anger: An abuser's goal is total control of another human being. Because this is an impossible achievement, his efforts are doomed to failure and his frustration and anger only intensify as he tries various ways to cage his partner.

There will be no rhyme or reason as to what upsets him, but the anger will be explosive and frightening. He may break things around you and threaten to do the same to you. You won't be able to disagree with him or question him or attempt to reason with him without invoking further rage.

On top of the escalating frequency of his terrifying, unpredictable outbursts will be his belief that your deficiencies are the cause of his behavior. If you would just become a better person, do what he wants, and show more concern for his needs, he would not have to act the way he does. He sees his behavior as your fault. Is it any wonder it can feel like you are losing yourself as the confusing, unpredictable "I love you – I hate you" illogical, emotional hurricane expands to fill every corner of the home. Your power and light are being chipped away each day as the abuse escalates.

In reality, an abuser is not trying to make his partner into a "better person." His goal is to create a robot that has only one goal: to serve him. It is impossible for anyone to live without interests, goals, fun, love, freedom, or safety. No woman can ever become what an abuser wants. No human being is put on this earth to be anyone but themselves.

In navigating the tightrope between the abuser's explosive anger and his constant criticism, it's common to find yourself walking on eggshells and rehearsing what you're going to say in a futile attempt to avoid his wrath.

Eventually, I believed that anything I said would evoke anger or criticism. The only thing that gave me any window of reprieve was to remain silent. Day after day I came home from work, cooked dinner, and went to bed speaking only when necessary.

Emotional and verbal abuse is terribly destructive, but it often goes unrecognized and unacknowledged for what it is. So many women don't believe they are victims of abuse unless it manifests itself in the form of physical cruelty. I was one of them.

Negotiation, compromise, and communication are methods used to work out problems in a healthy relationship. In an abusive, dictator/slave household, these tools are useless.

Bouncing between love and hate: One of the common themes identified in case studies of abusive relationships is how the women believed they could somehow do or become what their abuser wanted. Their goal was to prevent their partner's explosive behavior and maintain his affection and approval.

For years I, too, mistakenly thought such a goal was achievable. In reality, there is no connection between an abuser's thought process and his partner's conduct. A circumstance or behavior that upsets an abuser one day will be totally overlooked by him the next. It's a no-win situation. The constant fear this uncertainty creates is physically and mentally grueling and leads to a sense of helplessness.

My ex-husband's actions were so frustrating and unfair that I kept expecting him one day to "get it," to realize the cruel nature of his behavior. After all, doesn't everyone know that mistreating another human being is wrong? How could he not know this, and why didn't he stop it? As with all men who fit the definition of an abuser, my ex felt his outbreaks were totally justified.

Like so many women experiencing escalating levels of emotional abuse, the sad truth is that I was eventually brainwashed into believing I was at fault for everything, and I *did* need to become a better person. Commiserating with the abuser is one of a victim's final steps in an attempt to make the abuse stop.

Isolating you from friends and family: Once an abuser believes he is in a committed relationship, he systematically begins to enslave his partner through progressive programming and brainwashing. Because he is terrified of abandonment, his methods of domination methodically escalate in a desperate attempt to ensure his partner cannot leave. He sees anything and anyone outside his control as threatening, and as long as his partner maintains strong relationships outside the home, the abuser's power is limited. Therefore, he invariably seeks to isolate. To that end, he will attempt to prohibit his partner's communication with friends and family and destroy her emotional ties to others.

An abuser can make it so painful for you to visit your friends or family, either with him or on your own, that it isn't worth it. He may belittle you in front of others or make your life so miserable before and/or after you spend time with other people that the pain becomes too much and you just stay home.

He may monitor your phone conversations or emails, criticizing what you say. My ex would sit nearby when I spoke on the phone and listen to everything that was said. Before the call, he told me what I could and couldn't say. And heaven help me if someone asked me something he thought was too personal.

After a while, I arranged for my family to call me at work, and I made any of my calls to friends and family from the office. Cell phones and email didn't exist at the time, so I was glad to have a flexible office environment. Work was my saving grace during my years of trying to make the relationship work, as well as through the process of my divorce.

Eliminating your basic human rights: An abuser is devoid of the normal boundaries of respect that exist between two human beings. Since he sees you as a possession rather than a person, he believes it is his right to track your every move via the GPS on your phone or intensely monitor your whereabouts via text, phone calls, and email. He views it as his right to control or destroy your goals and aspirations, your activities and interests, your religious/spiritual beliefs, what you watch on TV, your access to money and what you purchase, the contents of your cell phone, what is on your computer, your choice of friends, when or if you see your family, what you eat and when you eat, when and if you can relax during the day, and what time you go to bed at night and get up in the morning. Eventually, the abuser suffocates every aspect of your emotional, mental, and physical freedom. (For more on this subject, see *Chapter 19 – Your Basic Human Relationship Rights*.)

It's More than Just Bad Behavior

Like many abusers, my ex was a highly functional individual outside of our marriage. Inside was another story. I finally began to realize that no matter how competent he was in his professional life, he exhibited a range of behaviors I labeled as "crazy" when it came to handling a relationship. I remember hearing loud and clear, inside my head: *One cannot predict or reason with crazy.* Little did I know how right I was. Over time, I learned that the characteristics and behaviors my ex was displaying were indicators of malignant narcissism (narcissistic personality disorder, or NPD) and sociopathy (antisocial personality disorder, or APD). NPD and APD are two of ten mental illnesses classified as personality disorders. The paragraphs that follow address four of these ten: NPD, APD, BPD (borderline), and HPD (histrionic).

For a long time, I thought *personality disorder* didn't sound like such a bad diagnosis, but this is far from the truth. The manual of mental disorders of the American Psychiatric Association, known as the Diagnostic and Statistical Manual of Mental Disorders DSM-5 (the number 5 designates the version) defines a personality disorder as "[a]n enduring pattern of inner experience and behavior that deviates markedly from the expectations of the individual's culture." Basically, personality disorders involve long-term patterns of thought and behavior that are unhealthy and inflexible, causing serious problems with relationships and trouble dealing with everyday stresses and problems. The DSM is used by health care professionals in the United States and is considered the definitive guide for the proper diagnosis of mental disorders.

Recent research from the University of Louisville School of Medicine reveals certain brain abnormalities common in people with narcissistic personality disorder, antisocial personality disorder (sociopathy), borderline personality disorder, and histrionic personality disorder. Additional contributing factors include childhood trauma, abuse, chaos, instability, or a family history of personality disorders.[5]

Chronic abusers with one or more of these four personality disorders do not know they have a disorder. They do not believe they have a problem, and therefore they do not seek therapy. Because of the common neurological nature of their disorder(s) and their inability to recognize their horrific behavior, they normally are not willing candidates for rehabilitation.

Like all personality disorders, narcissistic (NPD), sociopathic (APD), borderline (BPD), and histrionic (HPD) disorders cover a spectrum of behavior, and people with one or more of them can exhibit varying degrees of behaviors normally associated with their disorder(s).

Based on the DSM-5, descriptors of some of these behaviors are listed below. While some of these manifestations are truly bizarre, it is important to remember that *even behaviors at the low end of the spectrum are not normal.* Chronic abusers (the focus of this book) who have one or more of these four personality disorders commonly register high on the spectrum, which increases the difficulty of treatment.

Diagnosis of narcissism/malignant narcissism: In order to be diagnosed with narcissism (narcissistic personality disorder, or NPD), a patient must exhibit at least five of the characteristics listed below. The more severe diagnosis, that of malignant narcissism, is reserved for individuals likely to display all or almost all of them. (The DSM-5 does not recognize malignant narcissism as a formal diagnosis; however, this more severe presentation of narcissistic behavior, which is more likely to apply to chronic abusers, is recognized and diagnosed by many within the mental health community.)

- Has a grandiose sense of self-importance; exaggerates achievements and talents.

- Dreams of unlimited power, success, brilliance, beauty, or ideal love.

- Requires excessive admiration.

- Believes he or she is special and unique and can only be understood by and/or associate with other special or of-high-status individuals or institutions.

- Lacks empathy for the feelings and needs of others.

- Feels entitled to special, favorable treatment or compliance from others.

- Exploits and takes advantage of others to achieve personal ends.

- Envies others or believes they are envious of him or her.

- Displays arrogance and other haughty behaviors.

Diagnosis of sociopathy: A diagnosis of sociopathy, falling under the category of antisocial personality disorder (APD), is based in part on an individual exhibiting the first characteristic of the list below, along with at least three other traits from this list.

- *Displays a persistent disregard for the rights of others.*

- Shows indifference to the law, as indicated by repeatedly committing acts that are grounds for arrest.

- Disregards the truth, as indicated by repeatedly lying, using aliases, failing to pay debts, or conning others for personal gain or pleasure.

- Is consistently irresponsible, as indicated by taking impulsive actions without considering the consequences, failing to plan ahead, and/or repeatedly failing to sustain consistent work or honor financial obligations.

- Is easily provoked or aggressive, indicated by consistently getting into fights or physically assaulting others.

- Recklessly disregards his or her own safety or the safety of others. A sociopath may change jobs, homes, or relationships on the spur of the moment; exceed the speed limit or drive while intoxicated, sometimes resulting in accidents; consume excessive amounts of alcohol or take illegal drugs with harmful effects; and/or take pleasure in harming a partner.

- Doesn't follow up on personal or professional responsibilities, as manifested by behaviors such as being repeatedly late to work, quitting a job with no plans for another one, or not paying bills on time.

- Can feel little to no empathy, guilt, or shame. A sociopath exhibiting this trait feels justified when hurting, mistreating, or stealing from others, and afterward feels no remorse. Some professionals refer to this characteristic as a lack of conscience.

Additional symptoms of sociopathy that can be considered when making a diagnosis include: being unable to remain monogamous, being irresponsible and neglectful as a parent, using humor and charisma to manipulate others, being abusive to animals, being incapable of learning from mistakes, controlling others through intimidation and threats, and exhibiting an unreasonable and unwarranted sense of superiority.

The most egregious characteristics of sociopathy are varying degrees of a lack of empathy (a trait shared with narcissism) and a lack of remorse (conscience). Without empathy, these individuals can find pleasure in physical or emotional destruction of others. Many victims of abuse have lived with a partner devoid of empathy without being able to put a name to it. I was one of them; perhaps you were (or are) one, too.

It's hard to imagine not being able to empathize with someone who is in pain or going through a very difficult time. Even worse, think about what it would be like to have no conscience, no little voice in your head that tells you right from wrong; to feel no accountability for your actions; to never experience remorse, guilt, or shame. A sociopath lacking in conscience can feel free to do anything, no matter how heinous.

Although NPD and APD are each characterized by a unique mindset, specific behaviors, and spectrum of severity, there are several characteristics common to both. It's important to remember that at any given time, an individual can be diagnosed with several personality disorders. (See *Chapter 21 – Resources and References* to access further information on personality disorders.)

Overlapping characteristics of individuals with malignant narcissism and/or sociopathy:

- They believe you are beneath them.

- Due to their belief in their superiority, they have a huge double standard. Everything is for them and nothing is for you. Equality is not possible.

- They feel you exist to be exploited. They have no regard for your needs. You will be expected to take care of their needs and to make those needs your only purpose in life. You are expected to give up your life in order to please them.

- They can feel little or no empathy.

- They cannot be trusted to tell the truth. A healthy, enjoyable relationship cannot exist without trust. Lying is common in people with either of these disorders.

- You cannot reason with or predict the behavior of these mentally compromised individuals because they do not deal in a world of reality but, rather, in a world of smoke and mirrors. They are chameleons who adapt to the situation at hand, depending on what they want to get out of it.

- They have no regard for your well-being. Any pleas you may voice for better treatment will be dismissed and you will be seen as weak, further lessening your value.

Diagnosis of borderline personality disorder (BPD): According to the DSM-5, individuals with borderline personality disorder exhibit some or all of the following symptoms. Diagnosis requires that an individual show at least five of the characteristics listed within these descriptors.

- Makes excessive efforts to avoid real or imagined abandonment.

- Displays intense bouts of anger, depression, or anxiety that may last only hours or, at most, a few days. These may be associated with episodes of impulsive aggression, self-injury, and drug and/or alcohol abuse.

- Exhibits distortions in thoughts and sense of self that can lead to frequent changes in long-term goals, career plans, jobs, friendships, identity, and values. Sometimes people with BPD view themselves as fundamentally bad or unworthy. They may feel bored, empty, or unfairly misunderstood or mistreated, and they have little idea of who they are.

- Demonstrates recurrent suicidal behavior.

- Manifests transient, stress-related, paranoid thinking, or dissociation ("losing touch" with reality).

Diagnosis of histrionic personality disorder (HPD): According to the DSM-5, for someone to be diagnosed with histrionic personality disorder, they must exhibit five or more of the following symptoms:

- Is self-centered to the point where they feel uncomfortable when not the center of attention.

- Constantly seeks reassurance or approval.

- Has an inappropriately seductive appearance or behavior.

- Displays rapidly shifting emotional states that appear shallow to others.

- Is overly concerned with physical appearance, and uses physical appearance to draw attention to self.

- Has opinions that are easily influenced by others but difficult to back up with details.

- Engages in excessive dramatics with exaggerated displays of emotion.

- Has a tendency to believe that relationships are more intimate than they actually are.

- Is highly suggestible (easily influenced by others).

In addition, these symptoms must cause significant impairment or distress within the individual experiencing them.

Do you recognize any behaviors of your current or past significant other in the lists above? So many of us are or have been involved with one of these mentally compromised people without realizing it. Nevertheless, attaching a diagnosis to someone with a mental disorder *does not justify* and/or excuse their abusive actions. Abusers are always in control of their behavior. They have made the choice to abuse. They just don't see anything wrong with that choice, which is why they can't see the error of their ways.

Because people with NPD, APD, BPD, and HPD (categorized in the DSM-5 as Cluster B disorders) almost never see anything wrong with their behavior, they are not good candidates for rehabilitation. In the past, because they were seen as not being able to change, many mental health professionals and insurance companies would not provide or cover treatment for them. Even today, some insurance companies may refuse coverage.

Billy Eddy, LCSW, JD, is a lawyer, therapist, author, and senior family mediator at the National Conflict Resolution Center in San Diego, California. In June 2022, his article titled "Can People with Cluster B Personality Disorders Change?" appeared in the online version of *Psychology Today*. In it he states "there is no medication for treating personality disorders at this time." However, medications do exist to help patients who are also dealing with contributing issues such as depression or anxiety.

Although there is no cure for these personality disorders, greater understanding has led to ongoing experimentation with various treatment options, some of which have shown varying degrees of success. Borderline is the most treatable of the four personality disorders discussed above. Conversely, sociopathy is considered the least likely to change with treatment, though some inroads have been made with adolescents.

There are three main roadblocks to therapy for chronic abusers: (1) They need to see the error of their ways; (2) They need to seek help; (3) They need to commit to therapy that can last from one to five years, depending upon the diagnosis, with no guarantee of improvement.

You may be wondering if all abusers have one or more of the aforementioned personality disorders. The answer is no. Abusers can have other personality disorders, or they could be suffering from chronic and perhaps permanent disorders such as bipolar disorder, major depression, or a delusional disorder such as schizophrenia.

The mental health community cautions laypeople not to reach a one-size-fits-all diagnostic conclusion, first because we *are* laypeople and second because, in addition to a variety of personality and chronic disorders, there are other types of mental illness that can play a part in abuse. Unfortunately, unless abusers already have received a diagnosis (perhaps provided when they were much younger), we rarely have the luxury of a professionally rendered designation of their mental issue(s). And because abusive partners usually feel their actions are justified, they see no reason to seek professional help to obtain a diagnosis now. Given this reality, we have no choice but to come to our own conclusions regarding the mental health of an abusive partner.

How could there be so many of us who are or have been involved with mentally disturbed, abusive individuals? According to the cover of the book, *The Sociopath Next Door* by Martha Stout, PhD, one in every twenty-five people in the U.S. is a sociopath. Moreover, the DSM indicates that more than 10 percent of adults may have a personality disorder and 4.5 percent have one of the four addressed in this chapter. Sobering thoughts, indeed.

The bottom line is this: Mentally healthy individuals do not intentionally and consistently harm another. Trying to save a relationship with one of these mentally compromised men is not only a waste of time, it also can be very dangerous. If you remain in a relationship with one of these twisted individuals, you will be harmed mentally and/or physically.

When I finally recognized my own relationship for what it really was—a no-win, dangerous situation involving a mentally disturbed man—the revelation set me on the path to eventual escape.

Exhibiting extreme jealousy and accusing you of affairs: The jealousy you may have noticed while dating eventually becomes crippling. It is not limited to other men in your life but extends to anyone in your family or social network. An abuser sees them all as threats, so he'll do his best to isolate you from everyone.

He may even be jealous of the attention you give to your children and show it by ridiculing you in front of them.

Near the end of my marriage, my ex exhibited jealousy to such a degree that he accused me of having an affair with any man who talked to me. If we ran into one of my male clients, or if someone with whom I worked called me at home to ask a question, I had to face an avalanche of allegations. This behavior is a form of sexual abuse and yet another example of the absurdity and illogic in the twisted, disturbed mindset of an abuser.

Abandoning you emotionally: Because an abusive man views the woman in his life as a slave whose job it is to satisfy his every whim, he interprets her needs as an obstruction to serving him. Even illness does not excuse her from putting his needs first. In her book *Men Who Hate Women and the Women Who Love Them*, Dr. Forward describes how physical or emotional breakdowns are perceived by an abuser as weaknesses, confirming his contempt for his partner's deficiencies.

A few months after we were married, I caught a nasty cold that kept me home from work for a couple of days. I felt miserable, and I remember being absolutely flabbergasted when my ex returned from his office and got upset because dinner wasn't on the table. Nurturing, empathy, and emotional support are not part of the twisted mindset of an abusive man. In his mind, the woman exists solely to provide for him. Her state of health is irrelevant. In a healthy partnership, a man would either pick up dinner on the way home or prepare something for his ailing partner.

Minimizing, denying, and blaming: He will do his best to convince you that not only are you responsible for how he treats you, you are the cause of anything that goes wrong in his world. At the same time, he doesn't believe his behavior is anything out of the ordinary and will make light of it or even deny any mistreatment. This performance may take the extremely frustrating form of selective memory, literally rewriting history to his advantage.

Gaslighting is a term used to describe this rewriting of history. It originated from the 1938 play (and 1944 film adaptation) *Gaslight*, where the husband slowly manipulated his wife into believing she was going mad. Examples of gaslighting statements include "that never happened" or "I never said that." Even though you have proof, he might still deny it. He may tell you you're crazy or too sensitive in order to discredit you and invalidate your feelings. He may tell others you're crazy. The idea is to confuse you and make you question your own memory and sanity. This insidious form of abuse is a slow form of brainwashing.

In a good relationship, you enjoy the freedom to be who you are. A healthy union does not crush your life, it enriches it.

Impoverishing you: Abusers usually aim to take total charge of a couple's money, because money is a prime source of power and control. For example, he may refuse to share passwords to any of his or your joint financial accounts, keeping you in the dark regarding how much money he's bringing in or how the family income is being spent. You are not an equal partner; you are a possession.

It's bad enough to be excluded from this information on an everyday basis, but if he were to pass away suddenly, accessing any money would be a nightmare.

By completely dominating the family finances, he's making you totally dependent on whatever money he provides. Some women find themselves unable to purchase anything without permission, and/or they are expected to pay for all the household needs on whatever "allowance" they are given.

He may try to talk you into giving up your job or prevent you from getting a job. Some women have lost jobs because their abuser would not stop showing up at their workplace and causing problems. Once an abuser has successfully put you in an impoverished state, he has made it much more difficult for you to escape.

He may also look to you for money or take money from you. I know a woman whose husband insisted she give her 401(k) money to his alcoholic father, who was down on his luck. He had no right to expect access to that money. A good man would never have asked for it. She also had every right to say no. Sadly, she didn't refuse because she believed she'd lose his "love" if she did.

In a healthy marriage, authenticity is mutually valued and supported. Your partner offers a safe place to say what's in your heart and exercise your right to say no to any request without fear of the consequences.

Physically abusing you: When all else fails—and it will—the abuser will see no other choice but to turn to physical violence. When that still doesn't result in his partner becoming a robotic slave with whom he has vaginal rights, murder is the only option left.

Chapter 3

The Many Forms of Abuse

"Abuse manifests itself in behavior, and abusers consider abusive behavior not only acceptable but also justified—both a right and a privilege. . ."
—Thomas G. Fiffer

I stayed in my marriage for years: through continual emotional and verbal abuse, through control of my every movement, through isolation from family and friends, and through watching him break things around me. Why? Because I didn't recognize that his behavior was classified as abuse. After all, he was not hitting me. I believed him when he repeatedly told me everything was my fault. Therefore, I believed that if I tried harder, I could fix it. I stayed due to lack of education and because I was slowly brainwashed into believing my abuser's definition of me. It's common for an abused woman to believe she is worthless and to be terrified of trying to make it in the world on her own. I fit this bill completely. (For more information, see *Chapter 17 – Why Do We Stay?*)

What *Is* Domestic Abuse?

Domestic abuse is not a result of losing control; domestic abuse is intentionally trying to control another person. The abuser purposefully uses verbal, emotional, and/or physical means to gain control over his partner. The remainder of this chapter addresses the different forms of domestic abuse, along with behaviors corresponding to each type. Some of these behaviors may apply to your situation; some may not. Regardless of the form it takes, it's important to remember that abuse is *never* acceptable or deserved.

An article on the types, causes, and effects of domestic violence, published on the website of the American Academy of Experts in Traumatic Stress (AAETS), outlines the numerous types of domestic abuse, of which physical abuse is only one. The bulleted list below, as well as the remainder of bullet points in this chapter (except for those under "sexual abuse") are adapted directly from that article.[6]

- Verbal or nonverbal abuse (psychological, mental, emotional)

- Sexual abuse

- Stalking or cyberstalking abuse

- Economic or financial abuse

- Spiritual abuse

- Physical abuse (domestic violence)

Verbal or nonverbal abuse: Mental, psychological, or emotional abuse normally is characterized by shrewd behavior rather than physical violence. While physical abuse might seem the greater of two evils, studies have shown that emotional abuse can be much more damaging and have greater long-term consequences. This insidious form of mistreatment may include the following:

- Threatening or intimidating you to gain compliance

- Destruction of your personal property and possessions or threatening to do so

- Violence to an object (such as hitting a wall or piece of furniture) or pet in your presence as a way of instilling fear of further violence

- Yelling or screaming

- Name-calling

- Constant harassment

- Embarrassing, making fun of, or mocking you, either alone within the household, in public, or in front of family or friends

- Criticizing or diminishing your accomplishments or goals

- Not trusting your decisions or decision-making ability

- Telling you that you are worthless on your own, without him

- Being excessively possessive; isolating you from friends and family

- Checking up on you excessively to make sure you're at home or where you said you would be

- Saying hurtful things while under the influence of drugs or alcohol and using these substances as an excuse to say hurtful things

- Blaming you for how he acts or feels

- Making you remain on the premises after a fight, or leaving you somewhere else after a fight to "teach you a lesson"

- Making you feel there is no way out of the relationship

Sexual abuse: Since in the disturbed mind of an abuser you are a possession—a thing, not a person—he expects you to serve him sexually regardless of how he mistreats you or how you feel about it. He does not possess the ability to connect to your feelings, so whether you want to have sex or not is irrelevant to him. You have no independent worth. This is why so many women involved in abusive relationships are raped by their partners. (Marital rape is illegal in all fifty states. Sadly, this was not universally the case until 1993.)

Aspects of sexual abuse include:

- Demanding sex when you are unwilling

- Demanding or coercing you to engage in sexual activities with which you are uncomfortable

- Coerced penile penetration of any kind (oral, vaginal, or anal)

- Physically coerced sexual acts of any kind (e.g., through threats with or use of weapons or other means of inflicting bodily harm)

- Use of alcohol or drugs to obtain sex when you are (and/or would have been) unwilling

- Physical attacks against the sexual parts of your body

- Interference with birth control

- Insistence on risky sexual practices (such as refusal to use a condom when a sexually transmitted disease is a known or suspected risk)

- Exhibiting excessive jealousy resulting in false accusations of infidelity, monitoring phone calls, and limiting your contact with the outside world

- Forced or coerced participation in pornography

- Forced or coerced sexual activity in the presence of others, including children

- Forced or coerced prostitution or non-consensual sexual activity with people other than you and/or in addition to you

- Forced or coerced sex with animals

- Forced or coerced participation in bondage or other sadomasochistic activities

Here's the bottom line: Sex should be something you engage in freely, that supports you both emotionally and physically, and that leaves you free of guilt, fear, or resentment. You are not responsible for his orgasm!

Stalking: Stalking can take place during or after you have left a relationship. The stalker's goal may be to get you back, or he may wish to harm you as punishment for leaving. Stalking can take place online, via phone, through various forms of surveillance, or in person. Some stalkers may never show their face; others may be everywhere, in person, following you in a car or on foot. Regardless of the specifics, you will most likely fear for your safety. The following tactics are used by stalkers:

- Repeated phone calls, sometimes with hang-ups

- Following, tracking (including with a global positioning device)

- Finding your whereabouts through public records, online searching, or paid investigators

- Watching you with hidden cameras

- Suddenly showing up at your home, school, or work

- Sending emails; communicating in chat rooms or with instant messaging (see cyberstalking below)

- Sending unwanted packages, cards, gifts, or letters

- Monitoring your phone calls or computer use

- Contacting friends, family, co-workers, or neighbors to find out about you

- Going through your garbage

- Threatening to hurt you or your family, friends, or pets

- Damaging your home, car, or other property

If you are being stalked via the Internet or email (cyberstalking), the best response is not to respond. Treat cyberstalking seriously. It can advance to physical stalking and ultimately to physical violence.

Stalking is unpredictable and should always be considered dangerous. If someone is tracking you, contacting you when you do not wish to have contact with them, attempting to control you, or frightening you, report your situation to the local police immediately. Change all your passwords, particularly the one you use for the Cloud, and vary those passwords. Don't use the same one for everything.

If you are currently or think you may become a victim of cyberstalking, it's vital that you block your stalker from your social media sites, dating sites, and phone. *Before you do*, however, print a copy or take a screenshot of any communication you've already received. Google *WomensLaw* to determine if your state issues injunctions (restraining orders) for stalking and/or check with your local shelter to get help securing your safety. Google *domestic shelters* to find a shelter near you. You can also find information and help by Googling *Action Against Stalking* or *Fight Cyberstalking*. Fight Cyberstalking was started by Lisa Woeller, who was harassed by a cyberstalker from 2006 to 2018. Download her free "Fight Cyberstalking Toolkit." (See *Chapter 21 – Resources and References* for more help with technology safety.)

Economic or financial abuse: If an abuser can successfully put you in a situation with no access to money, he has made it much more difficult for you to escape. It is easier to isolate and place you in an impoverished state if he can talk you into giving up your job, and/or if he places you on "an allowance" where the only money you have access to is that which he doles out, and/or if he spends joint funds or incurs joint obligations in a manner that ruins your credit.

No one can know what the future will bring. Therefore, it is in your best interest both to maintain an independent form of income and to have your own credit cards and bank account. Even if you have joint accounts into which each partner deposits money for household or other expenses, I highly recommend also maintaining a separate account in your name only.

Financial abuse includes the following:

- Withholding economic resources such as money or credit cards

- Stealing from or defrauding you of money or assets

- Exploiting your resources for personal gain

- Withholding physical resources from you such as food, clothes, necessary medications, or shelter

- Preventing you from working or choosing an occupation [or interfering with your current job]

Spiritual abuse: Religious beliefs can be seen by an abuser as justification for expecting your subservience. Spiritual abuse includes:

- Using your religious or spiritual beliefs to manipulate you

- Preventing you from practicing your religious or spiritual beliefs

- Ridiculing your religious or spiritual beliefs

- Forcing your children to be reared in a faith you have not agreed to

Physical abuse (domestic violence): When other forms of abuse fail to cage you, the only method left to your abuser is physical violence. As he begins to think about beating you, he may threaten physical harm during his tantrums. Do not ignore his warning!

Once he does start to hit you, he may very well stop you from calling for help.

If he threatens to harm you or those you love, or if he has already hit you, call 911 if you are in immediate danger or call the National Domestic Violence HOTLINE, 1-800-799-SAFE (7233) to determine your safest and best options. You can also talk to the police and/or file an injunction at the courthouse. Choose what is best based on the urgency of your situation. When seeking help in a non-emergency situation, be sure to use a phone or computer your abuser cannot access.

Filing an injunction (restraining order) against your abuser may require that he leave the home. The local abuse shelter may have an attorney on staff and/or a presence in the courthouse to help you file. They also may have an office in, or a direct connection to, various police stations. If you would like their support, they can usually be by your side in the courtroom as well. They can help you, your kids, and perhaps your animals relocate to a shelter or a place where you will not be discovered. The HOTLINE will connect you to local services in your area.

Physical abuse is not defined solely by hitting. It also includes:

- Pushing, throwing, kicking
- Slapping, grabbing, punching, beating, tripping, battering, bruising, choking, shaking
- Pinching, biting
- Holding, restraining, confining [for example, using forcible physical restraint against your will, such as holding you down, trapping you in a room, or locking you into or out of the home]
- Breaking bones

- Assaulting you with a weapon such as a knife or gun

- Burning

Additional examples of physical abuse include withholding assistance for your physical needs, including help if you are sick or injured; rationing food or necessities; interrupting your sleep; denying you money or transportation; or forcing you to use drugs or alcohol.

When all else fails, the abuser may resort to his final option: murder. In many abusive relationships, the longer the victim stays, the more likely her life is in danger.

Each of us must make the decision to leave our abuser in our own time. But before we can, we must first give ourselves permission to do so. You do not have to stay in an abusive relationship. When you decide to take action, I encourage you to start by creating a plan for safely escaping and relocating with the help of the National Domestic Violence HOTLINE, 1-800-799-SAFE (7233).

I know it is absolutely petrifying to even think about leaving. So many fears are running through your head. How can my kids and I escape unharmed? How will I support myself? Will he come after me? What will happen to the animals? How will I find a job? Where will we live? How can I afford a lawyer? *You don't need to have answers to any of these questions in order to decide to leave.* That's the job of the domestic abuse support organizations. They exist first to help you create a plan to leave safely. Once you have escaped your abuser, they help you deal with all that's required to put you on the road to a healthy new life. And their services are free. *Shelters can provide so much more than a place to lay your head.* (For a list of services that may be provided in your area, see *Chapter 8 – Services Provided by Local Shelters*. Also take a look at *Chapter 7 – How Domestic Shelters Save Lives* for real-life stories of women who used the services of a local shelter.)

Because laws vary among states and sometimes between counties within a state, a shelter's connection to and/or knowledge of legal requirements and services in your area is invaluable. Reaching out for help is the first step. Remember, *you are not the problem*...he is. You're in a dead-end, no-win situation. No matter what you do, you can never make it better. You can never love him enough to make him sane. There is no security in a relationship that is no longer safe, supportive, or meaningful. (See *Chapter 5 – Why He Can't Change*, which includes insight into the mind of an abuser and why relationship counseling is not recommended.)

Manipulation through remorse: Do you remember the scene in the movie *Sleeping with the Enemy* where the abusive husband brings flowers and a sexy nightie as gifts for Julia Roberts after he has physically beaten her. After telling her how he hated to do what he did while simultaneously explaining that she was the cause, she was expected to put on the nightie and have sex with him (and she dutifully obliged to avoid the consequences). He believed he could beat her and still keep her by buying her something. I've heard this method referred to as "beat and buy." He had such confidence in his manipulative methods of apology that he was absolutely blindsided when she finally escaped.

When the perpetrator of domestic violence is successful in smoothing things over and convincing his partner that it won't happen again, his chosen form of manipulation has been successful. Sooner or later (often sooner), he will return to his old ways, knowing his partner will take what he dishes out, and a gift or nice dinner afterward will placate her.

In other words, no matter how "nice" he may be at times, *you are still living with an abuser. And he is never going to change!*

When my ex thought he'd crossed the line, he would keep me up at night for hours as he talked and talked. I could not go to sleep until he was convinced that he'd made it all better. It was like being interrogated for hours. I would finally give in just so he'd stop.

Coming home to dinner on the table and a gift was another method of apology he employed. By staying, I was unwittingly teaching him what methods of apology would work, giving him a green light to continue his cruel ways.

An abuser's theatrics and expressions of remorse are designed to suck you back in. He may seem sincere, but his intentions are *purely self-centered.* His desire is to quell the thing that most terrifies him: fear of abandonment. By using various tactics such as crying, begging, promising to change, gifts, saying he can't live without you, or making you feel you are the only one who can help him, he is playing on your sympathies, thereby shifting your attention back to him. Recognize these methods for what they truly are: forms of manipulation to put you back in his cage. It's all smoke and mirrors. If he threatens to hurt you, anyone you love, or your animals if you leave, call the HOTLINE and/or the police.

How Dangerous Is Your Situation?

Mosaic: A *free* software assessment called the MOSAIC Method (access by Googling *Mosaic Method* on your computer or phone) can help you answer this question. It begins with a questionnaire designed to help evaluate your current level of danger. An assessor uses your answers to weigh the circumstances of your present situation based on expert opinion and research, and compare them instantly with similar situations where the outcomes are known. The MOSAIC method works by breaking down a situation into its elements, factor-by-factor, the way you might break down a jigsaw puzzle, and then seeing what picture emerges when puzzle pieces are put back together.

If you feel your computer usage might be monitored, use a safe computer, perhaps one at the home of a trusted friend or a computer in a public place. Be sure the email address where MOSAIC will send your password cannot be read by anyone but you. If you're uncertain, obtain a new email address for this purpose or have a friend create an account for you using their information.

❧

Deciding to leave an abusive situation may be one of the hardest things you will ever do.
But remember: An abuser crushes your life.
It is not just okay to move on, it is your right!

Chapter 4

The Effects of Abuse

*"All conditioned things are impermanent—when one sees this
with wisdom, one turns away from suffering."*

—the Buddha

When you decide to take action to regain your life, you'll be
giving yourself and your children the opportunity for a safe and
wonderful future. You'll also be opening the door to releasing
yourself from any of the issues listed below that may apply to your
situation. Your family can take advantage of the free counseling
and support services designed to help you through the mental
and physical challenges of starting a new life. Call the National
Domestic Violence HOTLINE, 1-800-799-SAFE (7233), to find
out what's offered in your area.

How abuse affects the victim: As noted in the bulleted list below,
the results of domestic violence or abuse can be long-lasting. People
who are abused by a spouse or intimate partner may develop:

- Sleeping problems

- Depression

- Anxiety attacks

- Low self-esteem

- Lack of trust in others

- Feelings of abandonment

- Anger

- Sensitivity to rejection

- Diminished mental and physical health

- Inability to work

- Poor relationships with their children and other loved ones

- Substance abuse as a way of coping

If the victim does not leave the relationship, physical abuse may result in death. (Note that the list above, as well as the first paragraph and bullet points under the subheading "How abuse affects children" below, are taken from the article referenced in the previous chapter that appears on the website of the American Academy of Experts in Traumatic Stress.)[7]

Even if you are suffering from all or most of the above, you can heal. I say this because I suffered from eight of these issues and was able to find my way to health through trial and error. It takes time to heal, and in my case that time spanned more than twenty years of trying various healing modalities. In *Chapter 11— Releasing Yourself from the Past*, you'll find a list of the healing methods that worked for me. I'm hoping some or all of them will work for you, too, helping you heal much faster than I was able to.

How abuse affects children: Children who witness domestic violence may develop serious emotional, behavioral, developmental, and/or academic problems. As children, they may become violent themselves, or withdraw. Some act out at home or school; others try to be the perfect child. Children from violent homes may become depressed and suffer from low self-esteem.

As they develop, children and teens who grow up with domestic violence in the household are more likely to:

- Use violence at school or in the community in response to perceived threats

- Attempt suicide

- Use drugs

- Commit crimes, especially sexual assault

- Use violence to enhance their reputation and self-esteem

- Become abusers in their own relationships later in life

In spite of any harmful messages your kids have received by living in an abusive household, you can send them a new message of strength and courage by leaving. By leaving you are letting your kids know your marriage is not acceptable and you do not want them to ever find themselves in the same situation. You are stopping your sons from learning to abuse and your daughters from believing their value lies in the approval of and servitude to men. You are letting them know you won't allow yourself or them to be hurt any longer. As you rebuild your life, you're presenting a powerful new role model for both genders.

⊗⊷⥈⊹⥈⊷⊗

You and your children can benefit from free counseling that may be available through shelters in your area. Check with the National Domestic Violence HOTLINE, 1-800-799-SAFE (7233), or look for local support by Googling *domestic shelters*. (Be sure to use a phone or computer your abuser cannot access.)

Chapter 5

Why He Can't Change

*"Freedom is the open window through which pours the
sunlight of the human spirit of human dignity."*
—Herbert Hoover

*T*he mindset of an abuser: Dr. George Simon, whose PhD is in clinical psychology and who works with abuse victims as one of his many specialties, explains the thought processes of an abuser in an article titled "The Possessive Thinking of the Disturbed Character."8

> Habitual possessive thinking promotes a dehumanizing attitude toward others. When the disturbed character views others as primarily an object of pleasure, a vehicle to get something he wants, or a potential obstacle in the way of something he desires, it becomes almost impossible for him to consider them as persons with rights, needs, boundaries, or desires of their own. Viewing others as objects or possessions also makes it virtually impossible to acknowledge them as individuals of independent worth.

Abusers continue to resort to violence because:

- This method has been successful in solving their problems in the past.

- They have effectively exerted control and power over others through violence.

- *No one has stopped them from being violent in the past.*

As Dr. Simon explains, the twisted mind of an abuser does not see his partner as a person. This is one of the reasons why it's extremely rare for an abuser to change. To do so, he would need to see himself for the monster he has become; own his ability to abuse another human being; realize he, not his victim, is the one with the problem; and commit to a very lengthy course of professional help.

The National Domestic Violence HOTLINE website (www.thehotline.org) says this: "While we hope abusive partners will change, it's not realistic to expect that they can and will." The website goes on to suggest you focus on improving your own life. Despite what your abuser may have told you, you deserve to feel loved, happy, and safe.

In another article titled "Severe Character Disorders," Dr. Simon discusses the fact that effective treatments for such disorders are sorely lacking.[9] In an email from Dr. Simon received by the author in May 2022, he clarifies his thoughts on this issue in light of the most recent evidence available.

> At the present time, there are no clearly demonstrated effective treatments for severe character disorders. And there is SOME evidence that providing a certain group of severely disordered characters [with] the most commonly used empathy training information increases the risk that they will use that information to prey on victims more effectively.

Given the nature of their disorders, *these mentally compromised individuals do not wish to change, nor do they see any reason to do so.* In their mind, they see nothing wrong with their abusive treatment of others.

Moreover, even if an abuser *wanted* to change, he has neither the relationship skills nor the mindset needed to make it so. As hard as it is to imagine, he simply does not possess a normal human sense of right and wrong when it comes to intimate relationships.

Think of it this way: Expecting an abuser to be able to stop his behavior is like expecting a doctor who has decided he would rather be a lawyer to wake up the next morning with all the skills and education he needs to change professions.

Having respect for a partner is learned. Knowing how to appropriately deal with anger is learned. The ability to nurture is learned. Reconciling differences is learned. Knowing how to respect a partner's differences and boundaries is learned. Respect for the opposite sex is learned. Communication skills are learned. An abusive partner has learned none of these skills.

That said, it is not uncommon for a manipulative abuser to put on his "I'm-a-nice-guy" mask and morph temporarily into the person he presented himself to be at the beginning of your relationship in an attempt to re-ensnare you into his toxic cycle. Once he feels you securely under his thumb, he will remove the mask and abuse you again.

Expecting an abuser to change is both unrealistic and dangerous. When physical violence fails to mold you into the robot he wants, his next choice may be murder.

If I would have understood the impossible, dead-end, no-win situation in which I was living, I would have escaped years before I did. I'm hoping this information will help you to do the same.

Why Relationship Counseling *Is Not* Recommended

Just in case you're considering relationship counseling, here's some advice from professionals. Most experts are in agreement that it is the extreme exception for an abuser to seek therapy and to be willing to recognize and accept responsibility for the destruction he has caused and the monster he has become.

Susan Forward, PhD, specializes in therapy for abused individuals and has personal experience through her previous marriage to an abuser. On the outlook of successful treatment for these men, she says, "I wish I could offer more hope on this subject, but the unfortunate truth is that it is the rare misogynist who is willing to accept treatment."

Dr. George Simon puts it this way:

> I've counseled many disturbed characters over the years. All too frequently they reacted with extreme malice when the person with whom they had a possessive relationship tried to declare emotional independence. Sometimes, there were disastrous consequences when they decided that if they couldn't possess their partner, then no one else could.

It may surprise you that the National Domestic Violence HOTLINE does not recommend counseling for couples in an abusive relationship. To support this position, the HOTLINE offers the following on its website:[10]

> Abuse is not a relationship problem. While there can be benefits for couples who undergo therapy, there's a great risk for any person who is being abused to attend therapy with their abusive partner.
>
> Relationship counseling can help partners understand each other, resolve difficult problems, and even help the couple gain a different perspective on their situation. It cannot, however, fix the unequal *power structure* that is characteristic of an abusive relationship.
>
> An abuser may use what is said in therapy later against their partner. Therapy can make a person feel vulnerable. If the abuser is embarrassed or angered by something said in therapy, he or she may make their partner suffer to gain back the sense of control. Therapy is often considered a "safe space" for people to

talk. For an abused partner, that safety doesn't necessarily extend to their home.

Couples often enter couple's therapy to fix their relationship. Deciding whether or not the relationship is better is extremely hard for a couple if one is being abused. The abuser has all of the power and can no longer gauge if a relationship is getting better because he/she does not see what their partner sees. The abused partner often cannot even rate how bad or good the relationship is because the abuse has affected him/her.

. . .The facilitator may not know about the abuse, which would make the entire process ineffective. The abuser may make their partner seem responsible for the problems, and if the therapist does not realize that abuse is present, he or she may believe the abuser.

To this excellent list, I would add the following: Relationship counseling is not appropriate in an abusive relationship because abuse is not a communications problem. Rather, it is a problem stemming from the mental dysfunction of the abuser.

I wish I would have known this information before my abuser and I went to counseling. My own experience proved these predictions to be true. When my ex and I attempted relationship counseling, the results were disastrous and only added fuel to my ex's fire.

Why You Are Not the Problem

You are not the problem because *there is little correlation between how the abuser treats you and who you are.* He will abuse any woman with whom he is intimately involved. Her identity is irrelevant. Because he sees her as a possession, not a person, no woman will ever be acceptable to him.

With this in mind, do you think your abusive partner will ever find happiness with another woman? The answer is, emphatically,

NO! I so wish I would have known this very important point in the early years of my marriage.

━━❊❖❊━━

Give yourself permission to live an authentic life.
Make the call and find out what forms of support exist in your area.
Small steps lead to freedom and happiness.

Chapter 6

Your Safe Escape

"Stop telling yourself you can fix him. You can't.
He won't change. Save yourself instead."
—T. Ann DeCarlo

*T*he night I left we had both just entered the master bedroom and he was berating me because I had purchased a pair of jeans without him. I remember thinking, "This man is crazy and I need to get out now," and praying, "Please give me the strength to leave." I began to pack clothing, shoes, makeup, and bath products as he cried, thrashed about, and screamed at me to get out. Why was I able to leave unharmed? Why did he leave the gun in the drawer? Why didn't he take me apart right then and there? I have no idea and, at the time, I didn't care. I was numb inside. No matter what happened, I knew this horrible life was going to be over. I was not going to invest one more hour in a dangerous, miserable, totally impossible relationship. If that meant death, so be it.

Yes, I was lucky…. *very lucky.* I was isolated and lacked education about the severity of my situation. I didn't know about the organizations that could help me get out safely, didn't have a plan to leave under safe conditions, and didn't have any support because I had chosen not to confide in friends or family. My goal is to help you have all these tools in your arsenal when it's your time to escape to a new, safe life.

In the weeks and months prior to that fateful night, there were six things that began to wake me up and give me the strength and courage to leave:

- I finally realized I was in a no-win situation with a mentally disturbed man and he was never going to grasp how abusive he had become.

- All attempts to heal the relationship had failed and there was nothing left to try.

- One day, as I found myself wishing he would never return from his flying lesson—a hobby he'd taken up after deciding to build an airplane—I became aware that I actually hated this man and was actively wishing him dead.

- The fear of staying outweighed the fear of leaving.

- I began to imagine a new life, which was when I started to silently reclaim my power.

- He had crossed the line from emotional/verbal abuse to physical abuse.

How did he cross that line? The real jolt had happened a few weeks earlier, one otherwise "normal" evening when I was making dinner. By this time I was getting ill on the way home from work, fearing what might be in store. I said very little at home, since no matter what the subject, he turned it around to point out my stupidity or to accuse me of having an affair with any male client or coworker included in my story. That evening was no different.

I had come home from work and was silently making dinner. He came home and announced, "Now I know why my mother deserved what she got; she spoke back to my father." Then he added that if I spoke back to him, I would receive the same. This from the man who had once tried to kill his father for beating his mother repeatedly? I was dumbfounded.

I remained silent but—even though he didn't hit me—I knew his mindset had moved from emotional to physical abuse. I was now in danger of bodily harm. He'd played all the other abuse cards in his hand and still hadn't completed, to his satisfaction, the cage he was building around me. So in his mind, it was time to beat me into submission anytime I didn't meet his ever-changing requirements.

Until this point, I was telling myself stories I believed to be unquestionably true, stories about what would happen if I left or tried to leave. Stories like: Nobody will ever want me; I'll be alone forever. I'm not strong enough to leave. I can't leave the house that I love so much. I can't leave the animals that I love so much. I'll have to walk away with nothing. He'll come after me. I'll never get out unharmed. I'm trapped. There's no safe way out.

Did these stories turn out to be true? Most of them did not. Shortly after I left, I was able to secure an apartment, change my address, and arrange for movers. I did have to leave behind the house I loved and some of my animals. (Fortunately, I knew he would not harm the remaining animals as a way to hurt me.) My remaining fears, although legitimate, turned out to be far from true.

Regardless of the stories we tell ourselves, the real truth is that we all have the power to change our lives. No one is required or meant to stay in a destructive relationship. That said, you know your situation better than anyone else. No matter what advice you receive or how much your friends and family may want you to leave your abuser, *you* must decide the proper and safest time/situation to execute your escape plan.

Fear of the unknown and fear for our lives keeps us stuck where we are. I get it. Leaving an abuser is terrifying and legitimately dangerous, but I also know there is help available and there are ways to safely navigate through your fears and get out the door. For example, a temporary restraining order in your state may allow a mandate requiring the abuser to be removed from the home so you can pack what you need to move to a safe location.

(Professionals from your local shelter will normally help you fill out this paperwork and file it with the court.) Your state may also allow you to request a police officer be on hand for the removal process. Restraining orders have no filing fees, and help from the shelter is free as well.

More good news: Unlike when I escaped, there is an amazing web of organizations out there whose sole purpose is to help you. You do not have to go through this alone. I encourage you to give yourself permission to call the National Domestic Violence HOTLINE, 1-800-799-SAFE (7233). Use a friend's phone or another safe phone (one your partner does not have access to) and find out what help and support is available in your area. If you are in immediate danger, call 911. (Additional support organizations are listed in *Chapter 21 – Resources and References*.)

Obviously, I'm no expert on safely fleeing an abusive situation, which is why I encourage you to call the HOTLINE, where you will have access to those who specialize in providing this type of help. I will, however, tell you a few things I'm glad I did.

- **Maintained my job**: Although I considered leaving my job, I never did. Having the financial wherewithal to move on was a tremendous blessing.

- **Maintained financial independence:** Although we did have joint accounts, I'm glad I also kept my own checking and saving accounts, my own credit cards, and my own investments. What a blessing financial independence turned out to be.

- **Moved out while he was at work:** Moving out while he was at work was a successful but very risky decision. I hired a local moving company to transport my furniture as I frantically packed boxes and put them in my car. The movers had specific instructions not to show up at my house until I called them that morning to give them the "all clear." I was petrified my husband would show up during the day or that I wouldn't complete my packing before he returned from work.

If you decide to leave while your abuser is out of the house, I would be sure to create your safety plan via the HOTLINE before going ahead with this idea. Recruit help from trusted friends. Of course, their safety must be considered in your plan as well. I would also suggest calling your local police. Explain your situation and how terrified you are should your abuser show up, and ask for a policeman to stand by at your home until your move is complete.

- **Arranged to be out of town when the divorce papers were served:** Leaving town before the divorce papers were served was another good idea. He went pretty crazy and called everyone looking for me. I was able to stay away until the worst had blown over. Hopefully, your abuser won't know where you are if he is served with divorce paperwork. Perhaps you will have filed an injunction (restraining order) against him so he would be breaking the law should he come near you. Ignoring a filed injunction can result in jail time.

If you have filed a restraining order, keep a copy with you at all times and notify your children's school, their daycare facility, your work, and any other appropriate places that the order is in place. And remember to program all emergency numbers into your phone.

- **Rented a P.O. box:** Renting a post office box is a safer bet than providing the post office with a forwarding address when trying to keep your new location a secret. I originally provided a forwarding address, but the post office wrote my new address on my mail and then delivered it to my old home. The next thing I knew, my soon-to-be ex-husband was on my previously undisclosed doorstep.

I wish I would have obtained a P.O. box earlier, as it would have provided me with a location to receive confidential mail as I made new living arrangements.

- **Had my attorney escort me to and from the courthouse parking lot:** I was glad to have my attorney walk me to and from my vehicle on the day I had to appear in court. Women have been ambushed and killed by their partners before or after the proceedings scheduled to end their marriage. My abuser was particularly agitated and didn't hide it in the courtroom. After witnessing this behavior, my attorney insisted he walk me to my vehicle.

- **Arranged to be escorted to and from the parking lot of other frequented locations:** Arranging to have someone walk me to and from the car from places I frequented on a regular basis, like the gym, was another procedure that offered safety.

You'll notice I didn't mention obtaining an injunction (restraining order) against my abuser. I did try but, in those days, I could not file unless I had already been physically assaulted. I can't speak for the laws across this country, but I can tell you these laws have changed for the better in some areas. For example, the relevant statute in one state says "If you are the *victim of domestic violence* or if you have reasonable cause to believe that you are in *immediate danger of becoming the victim of any act* of domestic violence, you can apply for an injunction against domestic violence."

To see details regarding domestic violence laws in your state and the types of available injunctions (also known as protective orders or restraining orders), Google *WomensLaw*. In some states, you can even include pets in your injunction. To find out if your state is among them, Google *list of states that include pets in protective orders.* In many cases, you do not need an attorney to file an injunction, and there are no filing fees. You can file on your own, in person at the courthouse, or your local shelter will help you. Some jurisdictions provide the ability to file online.

A word of caution about restraining orders: They are simply a piece of paper, and they are ignored by many violent abusers. Several issues increase the likelihood of your partner violating the restraining order, including his having little respect for the law or abusing drugs and/or alcohol. It is important not to allow this legal document to reduce your level of vigilance or lull you into a false sense of security. However, if he does violate an injunction, he can be arrested. Huge perk!

Keep a record *that he can never access* of what he does to you or what threats he makes, including dates of occurrence, how you felt, pictures, what he broke, how he mistreated the animals, and how your children have been affected. Also be sure to keep appropriate medical records and anything else that will help the police and the judge see the true nature of your abuser. This information can be invaluable when you give yourself permission to start a new life.

VINE: Another service designed to increase your safety is Victim Information & Notification Everyday (VINE). This program was born in 1994 in response to the case of Mary Byron, a young woman whose abuser sought her out after his release, then shot and killed her. If she'd been notified beforehand that he was going to be freed, she might still be alive.

Before VINE, most victims had no way of knowing if or when their abuser was released. This is no longer the case. As of 2022, VINE is available in forty-eight states and covers more than 3,000 incarceration facilities. And while it initially focused on victims of domestic violence, today this lifesaving network is available to victims of all crimes. If your state/county is a participant, once your abuser is arrested and booked into the system you can access custody-status information on the VINE website and also register to receive automated notifications via email, text, or phone call. Google *vinelink.com* to access the website.[11] Some states take it a step further, automatically registering both the crime and the *survivor* with VINE. And some states use VINE to record the status of injunctions/restraining orders/protective orders, thereby allowing victims to know when an order has been served.

Since individual states use the service in different ways, once your abuser is in the system (even if you have just filed a protective order against him), I strongly recommend calling VINE Customer Service at 1-866-277-7477 to learn the particulars of how the program works in your state. Your shelter advisor or court advocate might be able to make this call for you. If your state or county does not participate in VINE, call anyway; customer service can usually let you know of alternative ways to keep up with the status of the incarcerated abuser.

Regardless of how VINE is administered in your state, it's important to note that *all interactions with the service are confidential. Your abuser will never know you have registered.*

Leaving Is Risky

Leaving an abuser can be very risky, especially during the separation period. Few abusers readily allow themselves to be left behind. Because the normal buttons they've pushed to keep you in line are no longer working, these men tend to escalate their methods of domination. Being prepared for his manipulative tactics will help you stand in your power and freedom regardless of what he does. In order to suck you back into his cage, an abuser may use strategies like these:

- Charm, affection, and promising to change

  - Offering to go to therapy (See *Chapter 5 – Why He Can't Change* for why relationship counseling with an abuser is *never* a good idea.)

  - Apologizing profusely

  - Attending AA or NA meetings in an attempt to prove he will stop drinking or taking drugs, or offering to enter rehab

  - Being kind to you, doing things for you, or making an effort around the house

  - Putting on the "nice guy" mask he wore when you first met, hoping you'll believe he can maintain this facade

An abuser in this "persuasive" mode acts sweeter than he has in a long time; he seems very changed; he stops drinking; he says he's really serious about treating you better this time. And it seems as if he genuinely means it. Maybe he does at that moment, but it won't make any difference. Abusive men who make serious, heartfelt promises to change don't follow through on these promises any more than abusers who make fake promises. Why? Because they can't flip a switch and miraculously become mentally stable, possess healthy relationship skills, gain respect for women, and be able to care about anyone but themselves. Would you ever expect a mentally disturbed person to be able to instantly heal his brain simply because he wants to act differently?

Remember, abusive behavior is a sign of selfishness, of an ownership mentality, of entitlement, and of a propensity for violence and power. It is *never* a sign of love.

- Guilt

  - Appealing to your sense of compassion by saying how lost he will be without you

  - Accusing you of abandoning him and ruining his life

  - Crying, begging, and/or pleading with you to forgive him

  - Threatening suicide

  - Soliciting other people to try to convince you to give him another chance

He acts helpless and victimized; he stops eating, stops taking care of his appearance, doesn't go out to do anything, and sends you the message (whether in words or just through his actions) that he can't live without you. He makes sure other people know how devastated he is and how much he loves you. He may manipulate friends or relatives into pressuring you by making them feel bad for him. Remember, his state of mind and his feelings are choices he has made. He is not your responsibility! Also keep in mind that gaining your sympathy is a form of manipulation, designed to make you vulnerable to becoming re-ensnared in his web. When you allow sympathy to override the reality of past behavior, you become putty in his hands.

After I escaped, my ex told wild stories to a shrink and a minister. Both of these people called me, convinced that my ex was a great guy and I was out of line. They had no idea of the truth. I don't remember how I responded, but whatever I said took them by surprise. I do remember thinking, "I am free and who cares what they think!" They didn't call again.

He doesn't let you get any space from him. He calls or texts constantly, saying he "just wants to talk" or saying, "I know it's over but I just want to be friends."

Here are some things to remind yourself of if he acts this way: (1) By refusing to respect your limits and boundaries he is still abusing you; and (2) If he really cared about you the way he claims to, instead of just caring about himself, he'd give you the space you need.

He's not acting this way because of how much he loves you. He's doing it because he's afraid and must get you back under his control and ownership. The "good guy" mask is back on, and it's the same form of manipulation that it always has been and always will be.

You couldn't make him happy before, so why on earth would you be able to make him happy now? As soon as you're back together, he'll only see what's "wrong" with you.

Your life cannot and should not be sacrificed to his. He believes you should give up your life for him. That's why the message that he's giving you now—that you should be with him even though you really don't want to be—is the perfect indication that he hasn't changed at all.

You do not possess the magic to change him. No one does. You do, however, possess the magic to build a new life for yourself, a life that's about you and your children and not about him.

- Fear

  - Threatening to hurt, kidnap, or take custody of the kids

  - Threatening to leave you broke and homeless

  - Threatening to hurt/kill you, anyone who is helping you, or any new man in your life

  - Trashing your possessions and/or your reputation

  - Threatening to kill himself

Abusers rarely carry through with the threat to kill themselves. However, if you go back to him, then you are, in effect, destroying yourself by voluntarily subjecting yourself to his many forms of abuse. Would you want your daughter or your best friend to return to a life of misery, pain, fear, and abuse?

If he's threatening suicide, the most important danger to be aware of is the danger to *you*, not the danger to him. Abusers who threaten suicide sometimes carry out very violent acts against their victims.

He may get scary or intimidating, showing up at places unexpectedly, making threats, or spreading lies about you. Through his twisted way of thinking and behaving, he says he's doing these things because he loves you so much. You may be able to file a stalking injunction against him or, in some states, your employer can file a workplace-violence injunction against him.

If his threats put you or anyone helping you in immediate danger, call 911. Depending on the laws in your state, his threats can have diverse legal outcomes. Several different kinds of injunctions exist to help protect you *and* to provide the ability to have him arrested if he violates them. As an example, injunctions available in your area may include risk-protective orders (to remove firearms), as well as protective orders against domestic violence, dating violence, sexual violence, and stalking/cyberstalking. Again, laws differ among states, but depending upon the laws in your area, some injunctions can remain in place for years. Google *WomensLaw* for a list of injunctions available in your state.

You also have the right to file a charge against your abuser for things such as criminal assault, aggravated assault, harassment, stalking, or interfering with child custody. Your local shelter may have an attorney on staff and/or they usually can help you obtain the legal counsel you need at little or no cost.

Work with the National Domestic Violence HOTLINE, 1-800-799-SAFE (7233) to make a safety plan for yourself. Make your own well-being and the well-being of your children, if you have kids, your highest priority. Call the HOTLINE often for frequent support and to strategize about the best ways to maintain your safety.

Once you leave, your abuser is likely to flip among tactics of charm, affection, promising to change, guilt, and fear in a desperate effort to regain control over you. It can be very tempting to succumb to some of his schemes. It's understandable to want to accept the charm, remorse, and promises of change at face value. Could he finally have realized the error of his ways? Could he finally be seeing the light? The answer is always *NO!* Remember, abusers are masters of seduction and manipulation.

If you find yourself inclined to believe he has recognized his errors and is truly changed, ask yourself these follow-up questions: Has he miraculously learned to respect the boundaries of another human being or how to handle his anger? Has he flipped a switch and overcome his lack of respect for women or his feelings of absolute entitlement to control you? Has he abandoned his unwavering belief that you are a possession belonging to him? Has his twisted mental state inexplicably healed?

No matter what tactics he's using to get you back, his beliefs have not changed, and if his manipulative methods are successful in convincing you to stay, he'll gradually go right back to his old ways and you'll find yourself living in hell once again.

Can you actually love your abuser? Yes, it is possible to love someone and at the same time realize they aren't mentally stable and are unsafe to be around. No matter how "nice" he may pretend to be at times, *he is still an abuser.*

What he is offering you is power and control, not love. Love is trust: safe, supportive, empathetic, kind, compassionate, respectful, and *fun*. By removing yourself and your children from the toxic environment created by your abuser, you're respecting yourself and opening the door to safety, real love, and a life of freedom and enjoyment.

You Are a Courageous and Strong Person for Leaving

Leaving is not a sign of failure. Leaving is not wrong. Leaving is *fixing* what's wrong.

Give yourself the enormous credit you deserve for deciding to leave. It is a tremendous act of strength and courage. The fear of staying versus the fear of leaving is very real, I know. However, the fear of leaving is temporary, while the fear of staying can be never-ending.

Courage is not the absence of fear. Rather, it is the act of moving forward *in spite of* fear. Removing yourself and your children from an abusive environment is huge and scary, but it is a necessary step on the road to a life of freedom.

Remember these words as you go through the process of escaping from your relationship.

- You can never love your abuser enough to make him sane.

- There's nothing you can do to change the life history that caused his twisted mental state.

- No matter what you do, you can't make it better.

- You can never give him enough love, care, or support or give up enough of your life to make him happy. *No woman can!*

- You do not belong to him.

- You are not responsible for his feelings or his actions.

- *You are not to blame.*

Living in fear is living caged in darkness. Leaving that environment is freeing yourself and your kids from a shackled life. You'll be free to make your own decisions, to do what you want, when you want, how you want, and with whom you want. The justifying, explaining, apologizing, walking on eggshells, and physical and mental damage will become part of your distant past. You will regain your voice and your power.

Ask yourself these questions:

- What advice would you give a dear friend, beloved family member, or your daughter if someone was abusing them like you are being abused?

- Would you *ever* do to anyone else what your partner is doing to you?

What would you really, really, *really* like to accomplish during the rest of your life? It's understandable if you don't know the answer to this question. As human beings, we can't dream when we're focused on survival, and your life has most likely been a frantic quest to avoid your abuser's unpredictable wrath. You haven't been on your own radar screen for so long that you may need practice at how to be good to yourself, to once again discover your talents and interests. (For help becoming you again, see the chapters in *Section Two*.)

After I left my husband, in addition to experiencing freedom from oppression and discovering enormous amounts of creativity and energy that had been suppressed for years, I was pleasantly surprised to find myself slowly experiencing freedom from physical problems. As abused women, survival has dictated that we suppress our feelings of anger, frustration, etc. However, no matter how successfully we have stifled such feelings, they don't just vanish. Sometimes they manifest themselves through physical or mental distress.

The connection between emotional stress and a variety of illnesses has been proven time and again. Depending on how stress has physically manifested itself in your body, you, too, may experience relief from symptoms such as muscular aches and pains, digestive issues, bowel disorders, headaches, and depression.

What Happens When You Call the National HOTLINE?

Everything you say during calls with the HOTLINE is confidential, and all services are free. The call will begin with them asking if you are safe right now and continue with questions that will help them understand your needs and provide the necessary help you require right away.

One of the services provided by the HOTLINE is assistance in creating a strategic safety plan with an abuse specialist. These safety strategies can involve two different sets of steps, one for increasing your safety while living with the abuser and another for formulating a safe plan for escape. When a HOTLINE advocate creates a safety plan with someone, the advocate includes information about the victim's local domestic violence resources.

These professionals can help with information about safe housing for you, your children, and your pets; counseling; and legal requirements. Services provided by domestic shelters are free. If someone goes to a domestic violence center and the center does not have facilities for pets on the premises, the shelter's service plan almost always includes an option to make sure your pets are cared for. Sometimes they have forged an agreement with a local facility to provide free pet boarding for a short time. Or they can refer you to a nearby shelter that does offer pet boarding. (See *Chapter*

8 – Services Provided by Local Shelters for a full list of services that may be provided by the shelter(s) in your area and *Chapter 7 – How Domestic Violence Shelters Change Lives* for stories of survivors who took advantage of various shelter services.)

If your local shelter has made connections with some of the police stations in your area, those stations may provide the ability for you and the father of your children to exchange your kids safely on police property.

The HOTLINE, 1-800-799-SAFE (7233) will work with you to devise a roadmap for leaving, helping you to bring some sense of order and structure to what for most women is an emotionally charged, chaotic situation. No one can guarantee your safety, but well-thought-out plans are vital to success. I encourage you to begin your escape by making the call and taking advantage of having someone oversee your safety while providing guidance and support. To find shelters in your area, Google *domestic shelters.*

Chapter 7

How Domestic Violence Shelters Change Lives

*"I survived because the fire inside me burned
brighter than the fire around me."*
—Unknown

*Y*ou may desperately want to leave your abuser but feel trapped for one or more of the following reasons: You don't have a way to support yourself and your kids; you believe you have no marketable skills; you have no idea how you'll be able to pay for legal help or where you're going to live; you wonder how and if you can protect your pets. And, perhaps of greatest concern, you can't see how you and the kids will be safe during your escape and thereafter. These are all legitimate concerns, but because of the amazing programs and support available through domestic abuse shelters, *you do not have to have all the answers before you leave, and you do not have to tackle these hurdles on your own*!

All shelters do not offer the same services, but all shelters have the same goals: to provide legal assistance and to be with you through the legal process; to provide a temporary, safe place for you, your kids, and your animals to live; to facilitate access to occupational training; to help you with relocation, if needed; to render assistance in your efforts to secure a job; to offer financial assistance and education; to arrange for counseling for you and your kids; and more. (See *Chapter 8 – Services Provided by Local Shelters* for a more detailed list of services that may be available in your area.)

The stories that follow show how shelter programs interconnect to help victims and their children break free from abuse and build new lives on their own terms. Sophia, Lori, and Monica are fictional compilations of the stories of real women from diverse backgrounds with a variety of needs. Rebecca is a real person who has chosen to tell her story publicly. All have one thing in common: the need to escape the chains of their abusers. With the help of shelter services, they were able to do so.

Sophia

Sophia was completely isolated. She had no family in this country and no one to turn to for help. Her husband had been abusing her for many years. Eventually, he started threatening to kill her. Although she was afraid for herself, she was even more terrified he would begin abusing their two children. Fearing for their safety as well as her own, she knew she had to take action. She also was desperate to find a way to protect the family's cat.

The call to her local shelter was probably one of the hardest things Sophia had ever done, but it was her first step toward freedom. Once she made the call, a wide range of services provided by the shelter helped her free herself from her abuser and go on to build a safe, supportive, and sustainable life for herself and her children.

Court avocation: Sophia had no idea how she would break free of her husband since he rarely let her out of his sight. To solve this problem, the shelter connected her with court advocates who helped her obtain a temporary injunction requiring her husband to leave their home. To keep her safe, a police officer served the injunction and removed her husband from the premises. Once he was gone, Sophia was able to get her family ready to move to the shelter. (A temporary injunction is granted very quickly for the safety of the victim. A permanent injunction is processed later.)

Medical care: Sophia had some lingering health issues she'd been unable to address because her husband hadn't thought they warranted medical attention. When Sophia mentioned her medical problems to shelter personnel, they promptly took her and her children to the doctor. The kids received a clean bill of health, Sophia's issues were addressed promptly, and the treatment was provided at no cost to her. (It's not uncommon for women, their children, and/or their pets to need medical care after arriving at a shelter, as some abusers refuse to allow family members to see a doctor.)

Pet safety: The children were especially pleased with the shelter's on-site kennel. Sophia had been so afraid she would have to leave the cat behind. Instead, the family pet had a safe place to live, and Sophia and her kids could visit whenever they wanted. Fortunately, the cat was not in need of veterinary care, but if it had been, the shelter had a fund available to cover any costs.

Childcare: Sophia's kids were still too young to go to school, but the childcare facility at the shelter provided a safe and loving atmosphere for them to stay for a few hours while Sophia worked on her case with shelter personnel and for the entire day after she found work.

Immigration legal services: One of the shelter's legal partners helped Sophia with her asylum application. Once it had been processed, she was issued a permit to work in the U.S. and soon found a full-time job.

Financial education and planning: Like so many abusers, Sophia's husband had kept her totally in the dark regarding their financial situation. By working with the shelter's financial coordinator, she learned everything she needed to know to handle her finances going forward. (Approximately 90 percent of all abusive relationships include financial abuse.)

Acquisition of housing outside the shelter: Sophia spent several months at the shelter. When she was ready to leave, shelter personnel helped her find appropriate housing.

Divorce legal services: With help from another shelter legal partner, Sophia was able to file for divorce and is now a free woman.

With a permanent five-year injunction in place, a full-time job, and a new home, Sophia lives a life free of abuse and her children are free from the tension and instability that surrounded them in their younger years. Someday, when they are older, she will tell them about all the help their family received, but for now, she simply tells them that calling the shelter was one of the best decisions she ever made.

Lori

Like so many victims, Lori was broadsided when her husband revealed his true colors. When they first married, he had mostly worn his nice-guy mask, taking her to fancy places and complimenting her on her organizational skills. When he asked her to quit her job at a local non-profit to help him in the family business, she was reluctant to do so, but he convinced her he needed her and she finally agreed. She soon realized this was a very bad idea.

Not only did her husband refuse to share any financial information about the business, he also became increasingly combative. The next thing she knew, she was drugged, beaten, and hospitalized. Meanwhile, he had been draining her savings, opening multiple accounts in her name, and running the business into the ground, all behind her back.

Lori spent several days in the hospital being treated for her injuries. As soon as she was released, she called the local shelter and took advantage of the following services:

Safety planning: Because Lori's immediate need was for safety, she was encouraged to meet with an outreach advocate. They worked together to create a plan for safely transitioning out of the relationship. Part of this plan included a temporary injunction requiring her husband's removal from their apartment.

Outreach services: Lori also received rapid housing assistance, which helped her find a new place to live. The shelter's victim-compensation program helped her with rent.

Financial assistance: Because her husband had annihilated every aspect of her economic stability, Lori also needed a financial safety plan. With the help of the shelter's financial coordinator, she was able to improve her credit score, begin the process of closing accounts her husband opened in her name, create a budget, purchase a vehicle, and secure a new job.

The call Lori made to the shelter was a critical first step. The services she received there helped put her back on her feet and leave the financial and physical abuse she suffered behind her. She is now living the life of freedom she enjoyed before she married.

Monica

Monica had no plans to leave her home when she decided to call the local shelter, but things were getting worse in her household, she told the counselor, and she really needed someone to talk to. "It's been going on a long time and he's never hit me, so I'm not ready to leave, at least not yet. After all, I'm not a spring chicken anymore. Maybe it will get better."

The counselor explained the insidious and often escalating nature of verbal abuse and the probable danger of Monica's situation. Monica appreciated the counselor really listening to her concerns, and she was relieved to learn she could contact the shelter again any time she needed someone to talk to. Over the next few months, she took advantage of the support she found at the other end of the line, but things at home continued to deteriorate. One day she woke up in the hospital with no idea how she got there. Her husband had struck her, but all she could remember after that was a blur of first responders, police, and flashing lights.

Her next call to the shelter, from her hospital bed, resulted in an immediate place for her to live within the shelter's walls. The safety of her new location and the restraining order the shelter helped her file against her husband resolved her immediate concerns, but they didn't stop her fearful, rushing thoughts about the future. She couldn't stay at the shelter forever. Where would she live when she left? How could she afford rent? Would she need a lawyer? Would she have to appear in court with her husband? What would a lawyer charge? And perhaps the scariest, was she too old to make a new life?

As Monica met with shelter counselors and talked with other residents, she learned more about the programs, partners within the community, and staff of experts available to guide her to a life of freedom. She also learned she didn't have to worry about associated costs for any help she might receive, since *all shelter services are free.*

Like many abused women, Monica felt she had mountains to climb to build a new life, but now she knew she would not have to climb them alone. As she took advantage of the services listed below, the rushing in her head began to subside and she relaxed for the first time in years. (Program names and content can vary from one shelter to another, but all shelters offer services to help survivors deal with past traumas and build strong futures.)

Support group for seniors: This group provided tools to help survivors rebuild their lives. Monica loved interacting with her fellow participants, some of whom were just her age. She was amazed how much she learned from the program.

Women in Transition (WIT): Monica also participated in this community-partner service designed specifically to help women transition from trauma to a new life. By working with abused women to identify and celebrate their interests, strengths, and skills, WIT helps survivors recover their power, creativity, and confidence.

Gardening program: While she was in residence at the shelter, Monica loved working in the large garden located on the grounds. The physical exercise helped her grow stronger in body and mind, and being surrounded by nature gave her a sense of calm she hadn't experienced in a long time. When food from the garden was part of a meal, Monica felt proud to know she was helping to heal herself while also helping others. Moreover, the money she earned in the garden program was a small step toward financial independence.

The gardening program at Monica's shelter had its roots in research related to trauma-informed care for women veterans, combined with studies exploring the restorative and healing outcomes of therapeutic gardens.

Court advocates: Monica was terrified at the prospect of facing her husband in court, both at the divorce proceedings and at the injunction (restraining order) hearing. She was so relieved to discover a court advocate would be with her anytime she had to be in a courtroom. Having someone by her side to explain the process and provide guidance gave her courage and helped her remain calm.

Outreach services: It was a wonderful day for Monica when an outreach worker found her the perfect apartment in the perfect place, a fifty-plus, multifamily housing development.

Financial services: At the time of her divorce, Monica lived in a 50/50 state, which meant she was entitled to half of the couple's investments and half of the money in their bank accounts. However, because her divorce wasn't scheduled to be finalized until two weeks after she had arranged to move, the shelter provided her with a security deposit and rent for the first month in her new home, a cozy, light-filled apartment.

Monica loves her new life. She is free of constant fear and is able to do as she pleases, when she pleases, for the first time in many years. She also is enjoying her new community and the many activities available to its residents.

Rebecca

Rebecca found herself and her children without any financial resources after she left her abuser. She applied and received money from the Soroptimist *Live Your Dream: Education & Training Awards*. These awards assist women who provide the primary source of financial support for their families by giving them the resources they need to improve their education, skills, and employment prospects.[12] With the money she received from Soroptimist, she was able to go back to school, earn a bachelor's degree in social work, and obtain a job as a social worker.

Google *liveyourdream*, then click on "Extraordinary Stories" at the top of the page to watch Rebecca tell her story in a short video. At the time the video was made, Rebecca was in her last year of studies for a master's degree in social work.

Each year, over $2.8 million in education grants is disbursed to 1,700 women through the *Live Your Dream Awards* program. Many of these recipients have overcome enormous obstacles including poverty, domestic violence, the death of a spouse, and/or substance abuse. Google *how to apply for the Live Your Dream awards* to find the application information you need.

Sophia, Lori, Monica, and Rebecca's stories demonstrate how survivors and advocates work together every day at domestic abuse shelters around the country. And remember, all shelter services are free to survivors and their children and all are completely confidential.

Whether you need safe emergency shelter, assistance with safety planning, help with navigating the legal system, training/help securing a job, or just someone to talk to, call the National Domestic Violence HOTLINE, 1-800-799-SAFE (7233), or your local shelter, which you can find by Googling *domestic shelters*.

———

Calling the HOTLINE is your first step to freedom.
One step at a time.

Chapter 8

Services Provided by Local Shelters

Remember: All Services are Free

Following is a list of programs and services that may be available at your local, state-certified domestic violence center.[13]

Confidential emergency shelter: These shelters meet immediate needs for things such as housing, hygiene products, and food for survivors, their children, and sometimes their pets. Residents have the opportunity to work with a case manager to make future plans for housing, safety, employment, transportation, childcare, relocation, and more.

Pet kennel: Some centers include a pet kennel, allowing survivors to bring their cats, dogs, birds, ferrets, and other animals with them. If on-site pet services are not available, the shelter may work with a local organization to offer pet boarding services.

Court advocacy: The center may have advocates located in the courthouse who can walk survivors through various legal processes with the state attorney's office, help create a safety plan, assist with filing injunctions, help apply for victim's compensation and relocation funds, provide referrals to legal aid, and accompany the survivor to court.

Legal assistance: The center may have an attorney or multiple attorneys on staff to represent survivors both in court as they seek injunctions for protection and at hearings for violations of injunctions.

Financial justice: Financial abuse and domestic violence often go hand in hand. Financial-justice programs equip survivors with knowledge and empower them to take control of their finances as they move toward financial freedom.

Child protective investigator: In some states, a child protective investigator (a government employee) connects advocates from the local domestic violence center with the government entity responsible for protecting children and families. This connection enhances family safety, creates permanence for children, reduces removals of children from the non-offending parent, and holds batterers accountable.

Children's services: State-licensed childcare services, including preschool and daycare, may be offered for the children of shelter residents. In addition, this area of the shelter may work with families to rebuild the parent/child bond that might have been damaged during time with the abuser.

Support groups: Group counseling sessions can take place frequently within a shelter. Support groups for domestic violence survivors may also be available in various languages.

Peer counseling: Advocates work with clients in person and over the phone. This counseling can take place at the shelter or in the courthouse and includes safety planning, crisis counseling, referrals, and assistance with filing for victims' compensation and relocation funds.

24-hour confidential crisis line: In addition to the National Domestic Violence HOTLINE, 1-800-799-SAFE (7233), your local domestic violence center may have its own number. For a listing of local shelters in each state, Google *domestic shelters.*

Google *SafeHavensforPets.org* for a list of organizations offering a safe haven for pets of domestic abuse victims.

❦

All domestic abuse organizations exist to
provide safety for you, your children, and your pets
and to help you regain your life.
Give yourself permission to make the call.

Section Two

*S*ection Two is for those of you who are in the process of leaving or have left your abuser and need to move on with your new life. Here you'll find information that it took me years to learn through trial and error, experience, and research. My goal is to give you a head start in untethering yourself from the past, eliminating its power over you as you regain your voice and your power; learn to trust and love yourself again or for the first time; and avoid duplicating choices that once caused you pain. As you work through this process to unearth your true self, you will become free to move into a life you love.

It's time . . .

– Donna Ashworth

There comes a day, somewhere in the middle of every woman's life, when Mother Nature herself stands behind us and wraps her arms around our shoulders, whispering,
It's time.

You have taken enough now. It's time to stop growing up, stop growing older and start growing wiser and wilder.
There are adventures still waiting on you and this time, you will enjoy them with the vision of wisdom and the companionship of hindsight and you will really let go.

It's time to stop the madness of comparison and the ridicule of schedule and conformity and start experiencing the joys that a life, free of containment and guilt, can bring.

She will shake your shoulders gently and remind you that you've done your bit. You've given too much, cared too much, you've suffered too much.

You've bought the book, as it were, and worn the T-shirt. Worse, you've worn the chains and carried the weight of a burden far too heavy for your shoulders.

It's time, she will say.
Let it go, really let it go and feel the freedom of the fresh, clean spaces within you. Fill them with discovery, love and laughter. Fill yourself so full you will no longer fear what is ahead and instead you will greet each day with the excitement of a child.

She will remind you that if you choose to stop caring what other people think of you and instead care what you think of you, you will experience a new era of your life
you never dreamed possible.

It's time, she will say…
To write the ending, or new beginning, of your own story.

Chapter 9

Awareness

*"The most beautiful stones have been tossed by the wind
and crushed by the water and polished into brilliance by
life's strongest storms."*

—Anonymous

*N*ow that you have left your abuser, internal healing can begin. Now you can focus on rediscovering yourself (or perhaps discovering yourself for the first time).

The first step in this process is awareness. However, for those of you who have recently escaped, the best you may be able to do at this point is simply put one foot in front of the other. I get it. I was on my own for about eighteen months before I could begin the internal work required for freeing myself from mental bondage. Don't feel pressured to begin. Wait until you are ready. If you need financial, legal, or counseling assistance as you set up your new life, I would suggest taking full advantage of the free services available through your local domestic abuse shelter. (For a list of possible shelter services, see *Chapter 8 – Services Provided by Local Shelters*. For a list of local shelters by state, Google *domestic shelters*.)

Many of us who lived with an abuser for an extended period experienced the equivalent of an emotional lobotomy. We completely lost ourselves in our ceaseless, futile attempt to avoid physical or emotional abuse and/or to placate our abuser. The essence of who we are—our needs, our dreams, our wants, our interests, and our personality—was psychologically and/or physically beaten out of us.

99

Whether we're aware of it or not, we've been brainwashed into believing, to whatever degree, our abuser's false, degrading, dehumanizing descriptions of us. Neural pathways in the brain actually change as this brainwashing takes place. Escaping the abusive relationship provides physical freedom but, as I discovered, liberating the mind is another story.

During my own recovery, I became aware of how parenting skills (or the lack thereof), along with the messages we received as children about the roles of men and women and society's definition of gender stereotypes, influence how we select a partner and, more importantly, shape *how we view ourselves*. Understanding these principles was like shining a light on parts of me I'd either forgotten or didn't know existed in the first place. This chapter contains the revelations that helped me begin the healing process. I hope you find them helpful as well.

Messages from home: It takes two to tango, an abuser and a compliant partner. Our patriarchal society teaches women to be "good girls." Anger, arguing, and assertiveness are not encouraged, and once I was involved in a relationship, I fell right into that role of "good-girl" obedience.

Parents and other family members can reinforce gender stereotypes, and my family was no different. For instance, when I objected to attending college, my mother told me I had to go in order to "find a man." The message was loud and clear:

- A woman is not complete or capable without a man.

- A woman needs someone to take care of her and, in my family, a college-educated male was deemed the best person for the job.

According to my therapist, my childhood was one of neglect. Both of my parents were amazingly functional considering their own demons: alcoholism for my dad and clinical depression for my mom. Each went to professional jobs each day and each was skilled and well-regarded at work. At home, they existed in separate worlds, interacting only to address household business. Affection between them was nonexistent, and this disconnect left our household devoid of nurturing.

Susan Forward, author of *Men Who Hate Women and the Women Who Love Them*, mentions how a father has the most influence in creating a sense of self-worth in his daughters. Even when a father is physically present in the household, his absence in his daughters' lives due to lack of participation, support, and guidance can cause self-esteem issues in his daughters and a need to look elsewhere for the affection they missed as children.

Growing up with this type of deprivation fostered my own low self-esteem and unwittingly caused me to look to men to fill that need for recognition and affection. In other words, I was primed to become the perfect victim, looking outside myself for confirmation of my worth and willing to be treated unfairly to avoid retraction of affection.

Repeating the familiar: I was surprised to learn how as humans we are unknowingly attracted to familiarity in a partner. Even if the parental figures in our lives inflicted considerable emotional or physical pain, we often are drawn to what we're used to. We're not aware of our subconscious mind saying, "Oh, here's an emotionally distant, self-absorbed man, hmm . . . feels like home." Familiarity is totally disconnected from whether one's background was pleasant or unpleasant. The familiar draws us in regardless.

I like the way therapist Robin Norwood describes this phenomenon on page 8 of her book, *Women Who Love Too Much*.[14]

When our childhood experiences are particularly painful, we are often unconsciously compelled to recreate similar situations throughout our lives, in a drive to gain mastery over them.

To this end, we are attracted to men who replicate the struggle we endured with our parents when we tried to be good enough, loving enough, worthy enough, helpful enough, and smart enough to win the love, attention, and approval from those who were not capable of giving us what we needed.

We can be unaware that we're operating as though love, attention, and approval don't count unless we are able to extract them from a man who is also unable to readily give them to us. Accustomed to lack of love in personal relationships, we are willing to wait, hope, and try harder to please.

This revelation was a big eye-opener. Like my dad, my ex-husband was an engineer. Outside of my ex's work, he existed in a world of big-boy toys, spending his leisure hours building a boat and an airplane. Like his abusive father, my ex made no time in his world for family or relationships. Lacking any relationship skills, he replicated, in an exaggerated, abusive form, the familiar neglect with which I was raised. Because he was a college-educated man who had the means to "take care of me," he also fulfilled the message I'd received from my mother.

Messages from an abusive household: Society's message of male entitlement and female submission is taken to the extreme in an abusive household. Children raised in this environment are victims on a much greater scale. What they endure—and the resulting unquestioned messages they take with them into adulthood—can lead them to become perpetrators of the very situations they hated as children.

In *Men Who Hate Women and the Women Who Love Them*, Susan Forward states, "For the last 10 years I have specialized in working with adults who were victims of various forms of abuse as children. I have found no other life event so scars people's self-esteem or sets them up for major emotional difficulties in adulthood."

Women raised in an abusive environment are subject to messages such as these:

- Submission is the only way to handle an aggressive man.

- Men have the freedom to do anything they want and treat a woman any way they want, and a woman has to submit to the man's wishes.

- A woman must tolerate whatever treatment her partner dishes out in order to maintain the relationship.

- A woman must have a relationship with a man, no matter what the cost to herself or her children.

- Love is synonymous with tension, drama, chaos, anger, and control.

A woman who is unaware of these subconscious, unrealistic beliefs, often formed during childhood, can find herself in hellish relationships simply because they feel familiar.

Media's Toxic Messages

A woman's power lies in her body: When it comes to acknowledging women as intelligent, capable human beings, our society has failed miserably. We are constantly bombarded by messages that *women are valued for being ornaments and sexual objects*. All forms of media project images of women with "perfect" Photoshopped bodies, dressed in revealing clothing. If anything, it seems like such messages are growing stronger as it becomes more acceptable for women to wear less.

Can you recall a scene from any movie that is set in the tropics, such as *Medicine Man*, where a male and female are trudging through the jungle? The man is dressed in appropriate protective clothing for the environment. The woman is wearing hiking boots, buttocks-revealing shorts, and a white, see-through, low-cut tank top.

It's common for women in business roles on TV shows to be dressed in skin-tight skirts or painted-on pants and tops that reveal considerable cleavage. When was the last time you saw a TV show or movie where the businessmen walked about their office with their starched dress shirts unbuttoned to the navel, revealing their chests? If they did, it would be hard to view them as professionals or take them seriously, wouldn't it?

The plot of television shows like *Hot in Cleveland* revolved around women trying to find men to fix their lack of happiness and fulfillment.[15] The women were depicted as being miserable and unhappy because they were single. Every episode focused on their various attempts to secure a relationship.

You may be thinking, "Oh come on… *Hot in Cleveland* was just a situation comedy." True but, surprisingly, humor is a very powerful means of communicating a message.

So many TV shows and movies portray our society's tacit acceptance of male entitlement. Once involved in a relationship, the woman gives away her power, deferring decisions to the man. The relationship becomes more father/daughter-like, since whatever the man wants goes. If he wants something, she defers to his decision and he gets it. If she wants something and he disagrees, she defers to his decision and she doesn't get it.

This message of subservience, provided in massive doses throughout the media, encourages women to defer to others for approval. Without a man, we are not encouraged to see ourselves as competent, self-sufficient adults; to feel comfortable in our own skin; or to trust in our own wisdom. Our role is reduced to that of eye candy.

I'll never forget the story one woman told me about a stray, starving, pregnant cat that showed up at her family's home. Her husband ordered her not to feed it. She watched as this starving animal would do its best to beg for food but could barely stand long enough to do so. She was this cat's last hope. Finally, her instincts outweighed her fear of disobeying her husband's heartless command and she began to care for the helpless creature, eventually nursing it back to full health. Ironically, the cat became a beloved member of the family.

What's so sad about this story is that it never occurred to this woman that she had any vote (let alone 50 percent) in the decision-making dynamic in her own household. Negotiation wasn't an option. Because she did not stand in her power and see herself as an equal partner, she had to deal with the consequences (anger, arguments, etc.) of usurping her husband's accepted authority in order to save the cat.

This couple's relationship was not necessarily one of abuse; it may simply have been one of unquestioned inequality. Both husband and wife bought society's insidious "brule" (bull**** rule) that the man is running the show and the woman is subservient to his wishes as soon as they become a couple. This concept of male entitlement has been ingrained in our culture for so long that it frequently goes completely unnoticed by both genders. In this case, the couple was not only unaware of the bizarre nature of their mindset, they were unwittingly passing it down to their children.

Perpetuating the inequality of women in our society continues to breathe life into abuse.

Some music videos and computer games graphically portray hypersexualized women with aggressive men in control. Certain songs and the corresponding videos that boldly discuss and portray the abuse of women have won prestigious awards.

The overwhelming, unavoidable messages being shouted from far too many magazines, movies, Internet sites, songs, and television shows are:

- A woman's power is external and based solely on how she is seen through the eyes of men.

- A woman is a sex toy.

- A woman's role in this world is that of an ornament.

- Women exist to serve men.

- A woman's life is incomplete and miserable without a man.

- Men are the decision-makers.

- Women are inferior and should be subservient to men.

- Men are entitled to control and power.

A woman's unaltered appearance is always inadequate: Advertisers are making billions with the message *"You aren't good enough or pretty enough as you are."* Their goal is to make the female audience feel disempowered, empty, and defective. Of course, by purchasing the right product or having surgery, women can fix their "flaws" and be made "whole" and worthy of love again.

Is there any part of a woman's body that has not been scrutinized and exploited for profit? Hair, eyelashes and eyebrows, skin, lips, teeth, cheekbones, chin, ears, neck, upper arms, hands, nails, breasts, waist, stomach, back, buttocks, thighs, knees, calves, ankles, and feet. Some women have even had cosmetic surgery on their labia and vagina, not because of any medical necessity but strictly to please a man. It's no wonder both genders unconsciously buy the "women-need-fixing" message lock, stock, and barrel. It's everywhere.

As loud and enveloping as this directive has become in our electronic age, it all too often goes undetected. Granted, it is not a new message. Women have always been treated as second-class citizens, but multimedia's constant reinforcement of women's objectification has exacerbated an already damaged, and damaging, environment.

To some degree, we all unconsciously absorb and act on these ubiquitous messages. And irresponsible advertisers count on us to remain oblivious pawns in their money sport. Various media forms, but particularly TV, show how many women mentally and physically beat themselves up for not being able to reach the unobtainable image of the perfect, Photoshop-enhanced, magazine-cover body. One can imagine their unconscious thought process: *I am not physically perfect; therefore, I am not worthy of love. I will starve myself, put whatever chemical-laden creams and potions on my body to perfect my skin, inject whatever it takes to remove wrinkles, and have as many plastic surgeries as I can afford to fix my "flaws." Only then will I be acceptable in the eyes of men and worthy of love.* Lack of self-approval can express itself in eating disorders, self-mutilation, and/or depression.

The documentary *Miss Representation*, written, directed, and produced by Jennifer Siebel Newsom, shines a huge light on how media's toxic messages affect women in our society.[16] For teenage girls and women of any age, it is a true eye-opener.

I wholeheartedly and unconsciously internalized the mass media message, which manifested itself in me as an eating disorder and two plastic surgeries. I expected to somehow feel transformed into wholeness by these external changes and was confused when it didn't happen. Why? Because the message *"appearance equals self-worth"* is inherently defective.

No amount of approval from the outside world will be meaningful unless one is comfortable in one's own skin. In other words, self-worth comes from the inside, not the outside. We can nip, tuck, and starve our bodies from now to the end of time, but it won't change the fact that our value lies in acceptance and love of ourselves.

Awareness of media-induced exploitation helps build internal strength. By taking our brains off autopilot and rejecting advertisers' manipulative attempts to brainwash us for monetary gain, we redeem our power to make our own choices. When our emotional well-being is no longer tied to the whims of others, we regain our ability to act in our own best interests.

The connection between society's message on the role of the sexes and domestic abuse: Society's message regarding roles and expectations based on gender is one more ingredient in the recipe for creating a victim or an abuser. A woman who externalizes her power, looking to a man for her sense of self-worth, is very vulnerable. This vulnerability, layered on top of an upbringing of control, neglect, and/or abuse greatly increases her likelihood of accepting an abusive partner.

The general suppression of females is fueled by men who have internalized society's message that they are superior to women and that women exist for their pleasure. To the man with abusive tendencies, these messages can be one more form of corroborating support that cruelty and exploitation of his partner is his right.

Chapter 10

Awakening

"" If you want to fly, give up everything that weighs you down."
—the Buddha

The previous chapter opened the door to the various origins of unquestioned self-deprecating thoughts—media messages that have become unconscious "truths"; old, unreasonable childhood beliefs; and your abuser's repeated, false, degrading characterization of you. This chapter offers encouragement to pursue an understanding of and trust in yourself, to uncover who you truly are.

Research has shown that the more we realize what shaped us as individuals, the more resources we have to break free of thoughts, beliefs, and actions that no longer serve us. More importantly, the greater our insight, the greater our power to break the cycle of choosing abusive partners.

As you work on getting to the truth of *who you are* and *what you believe*, small changes will begin to take place in your brain, changes that override untrue and detrimental thoughts. This transition is not a rapid process, since many of these thoughts have existed unchallenged since childhood, and the repetitive nature of verbal abuse causes its own changes in the brain as self-esteem is systematically eroded.

Do you find yourself believing wholeheartedly that you're selfish, ugly, fat, incapable, socially inept, lazy, stupid, or any other descriptions heaped on you by your abuser and/or absorbed as truth from your childhood? I know I did. I felt so flawed that no matter where I went, I was convinced that anyone who looked at me knew I was a terrible person. In reality, my ex-husband was describing himself when he labeled me so negatively. It took a psychologist to point out this fact before I could see it. The therapist explained that it was my husband who was being unconscionably selfish and embodying all the negative characteristics he was heaping on me. What a revelation! Perhaps this awakening applies to your situation, too.

When we finally are able to let go of these thought patterns from the past, we reclaim our power, our voice, our value and our values, our imagination, our creativity, our courage, our strength, our joy, our sense of self, our ability to trust our decisions, our understanding that we are worthy of love, our capacity to love, our authenticity, and the determination to allow only those who support us into our lives.

I can't stress enough the importance of focusing on cultivating a relationship with your new and true self before considering a relationship with another. Those who do not take the time to understand and truly embrace themselves are very likely to duplicate unhealthy and dangerous relationships. We choose the same type of partner unless we become aware of and nurture our wounds.

In other words, you have to believe you are wonderful before you can accept someone who feels the same way about you. Conversely, you'll have a hard time accepting someone into your life who thinks you're good enough if you think you are not.

It's okay to be the center of your world. You deserve all the time and attention it takes to say yes to you. We're not taught the importance of discovering who we really are and of caring for ourselves. Once we finally "get this," it makes a mammoth difference.

Put another way, once you fully understand yourself, you eventually will be able to accept your negative experiences and move on from them. This self-understanding also can foster a deeper connection with your children. Keep in mind that coherent self-knowledge goes hand in hand with healthy interpersonal relationships.

Traveling this journey is likely to generate intense feelings and memories. I encourage you to engage good friends to be there for you when you need someone to listen and inspire you to keep working through the healing process.

Years of domestic abuse and violence can result in post-traumatic stress disorder (PTSD), a persistent and distorted sense of self-blame, the inability to connect with others, depression, substance abuse, sleeping problems, a lack of trust in others, feelings of abandonment, anger, sensitivity to rejection, diminished mental and physical health, and a lack of self-esteem. I suffered from and needed to address all but two of these issues. *Chapter 12 – Methods that Helped Me Heal* outlines the methods I used to do so successfully. Hopefully, you may find some or all of these methods helpful as well.

Chapter 11

Releasing Yourself from the Past

"Life is better on the high road. To stay there requires that we pay attention as we move through each day, and that's considerably easier, more productive, and way more fun than chasing the ghosts of the past."
—John B. Waterhouse

When the time is right for you, it is imperative that you mentally untether yourself from your abuser and the things he did to you. Cutting the memory cords that still give him power over you is a critical step to freedom as you move forward in your new life.

Releasing or untethering yourself from unpleasant memories has nothing to do with the person or persons who have mistreated you. It doesn't mean you condone their actions or that you have anything to do with them. The untethering process is solely for you and solely about you. It offers the freedom that unburdens you and sets you firmly on the path to rebirth in the form of a new life and a new way of being. It ultimately brings peace.

You have been mentally, emotionally, verbally, and perhaps physically assaulted by your abuser, and you carry with you the associated pain, misery, fear, judgment, and blame. Your abuser deserves all the pain you're carrying with you; you don't.

What has been done to you has left a very, very deep mental wound. Releasing yourself from the past is an important part of the healing process. I wouldn't have included this advice if I hadn't experienced this release myself. I remember feeling that the only way out of the pain, fear, and misery that consumed me after I'd escaped would be if my abuser no longer existed on this earth. I believed he didn't deserve to live long enough to do to anyone else what he had done to me, and that the planet would be better off without him. His demise would be appropriate justice, provide me with great happiness, and set me free. Many years later, I know that if my wish would magically have been granted, my wounds and the corresponding pain, fear, and misery would have remained.

I also spent thousands of hours wishing I'd stood up to him, imagining how things might have been had I put him in his place and never accepted any of the mistreatment I withstood silently. So many imaginary conversations. I've learned since, however, that standing up to an abuser can have devastating results, and I don't recommend it. I've also come to realize that my repetitive thoughts of self-recrimination were, in fact, another form of suffering, only this time self-inflicted. I didn't understand that by clinging to the pain and fault-finding stories of my past, not only was I denying my true nature, I was disempowering myself.

Had I known I had the ability to set myself free and move on, I could have redirected all the energy I wasted on endless scenarios of woulda, coulda, shoulda to adding joy to my life. I don't want you to make the same mistakes I did. I don't want you to allow your abusive past to live with you, truncate your life, take your time, or hold you back.

That said, it's important to appreciate that peace is an inside job. Acknowledging the control you have over your thoughts is the first step to leaving behind the baggage you've accumulated from years of abuse. It doesn't change what happened, but it enables you to let go of the rage you feel toward your abuser and what he did. This is the beauty of untethering. It dissolves any sense of being a victim and reestablishes you as master of your earthly experiences. Over time, your memory can reach a neutral state where what he did no longer affects you, and where thinking about the past no longer generates an emotional charge.

Your abuser's twisted mind will never allow him to experience the fulfillment of a good relationship. To open yourself to the full range of your own potential, you must love yourself enough to break the mental cables that keep you bound to your abuser and to your previous experiences. In the end, the greatest revenge is living a great life.

I realize this is far easier said than done. You can't just flip a switch, stop thinking about what he did to you, and instantly put it behind you. This journey takes time and effort. I began by trying to understand how my ex became an abuser. (See *Chapter 18 – The Making and Mindset of an Abuser* for more on this subject.) What I learned helped me start the releasing process. It did not invoke sympathy in me for my abuser, but I found the information helpful.

Nurturing positive thoughts: Having learned I can be the observer of my thoughts and control how and what I choose to think, I now catch myself when I fall into old habits. If I find myself beginning to run a tape of something that happened during my marriage, I say STOP and change my focus to something positive happening in my life today.

Paying attention to our thoughts can be extraordinarily revealing.

It takes time and repetition to create the damaging tapes that run in our heads. Replacing these negative reruns with new tapes works the same way. A new tape can be something as simple as "I love my fresh and wonderful life" or "I am an intelligent, capable, and kind person." Pick statements that work for you and switch to the appropriate thought each time you find yourself reliving a scenario from your abusive relationship. Just give it time and know you are taking control!

Journaling is another method that helps leave the past in the past. A journal offers a safe place to say anything you want without being judged, criticized, or dismissed. I found (and continue to find) the process tremendously comforting. Write out all your feelings about what happened to you; spew everything onto the paper. Get it all out as many times as you need to. And don't forget to write about how brave you were to escape the abuse and what you learned from your experience. All experiences, even those as horrible as what we've lived through, offer valuable lessons and call us to affirm that we are incredibly powerful and that we are capable of moving on to happy, meaningful, and productive lives.

As you experience untethering and the positive power it has on your life, you'll begin to notice those around you who haven't let go of the past. For example, a man approached my girlfriends and me at a restaurant where we were celebrating one girlfriend's divorce. He immediately told us he had been divorced for three years and provided a detailed, angry description of how his wife did him wrong. Not only was it immediately apparent that he was not able to see or admit his participation in the demise of the relationship, his comments further revealed he was still clinging to the pain and fault-finding of his divorce.

In my distant past I may have felt sorry for this man and wanted to come to his rescue, but not anymore. The hypervigilance and discernment born of self-love, releasing the past, and becoming conscious of who I am has provided the gift of clarity. Instead of seeing someone who needed saving, my friends and I knew he needed to come to terms with himself and his past. Until he did so, he would simply repeat the same mistakes. Can you see how his anger still tethered him to his past marriage and how his inability to acknowledge any fault leading to the demise of the partnership would get in the way of forming a healthy new relationship and having a fulfilling life?

Like unwanted boarders, pain and hurt from the past take up space in our lives. Once we are able to let them go, we can fill that space with loving people and fabulous experiences. (See *Chapter 12 – Methods that Helped Me Heal* for techniques I used to release thoughts and memories that did not serve me.)

Forgiving Yourself

At one point during my process of healing, I realized the anger I was feeling was no longer aimed at my abuser. Rather, I was upset with myself. Why did I put up with his crap? Why didn't I leave years earlier? Why didn't I tell him what a horrible person he was? I'm sure I'm not the only one out there who has, has had, or will have these same self-deprecating feelings.

Anytime you have thoughts like these, I want you to remember that you were doing the best you could with the knowledge you possessed at the time. Plus, confronting an abuser can have devastating results. No matter how satisfying you think it might feel, I don't recommend it!

We become very different people as we move on. We can't berate ourselves for not knowing then what we know now, for not being the older and wiser people then that we have since become. You need not have any guilt or shame about who you were in the past. Remember, you have chosen to be free, the clear alternative to remaining a victim. You left, you've grown, you've learned what didn't work, you've opened yourself to a new world full of possibilities, and you've regained control of your life. *Bravo!*

Chapter 12

Methods that Helped Me Heal

"We teach others how to treat us. When we respect and love ourselves, we will accept nothing less from another."
—T. Ann DeCarlo

*T*he previous chapter stressed the importance of untethering yourself from your abusive past. Cutting any remaining mental ties to your abuser eliminates his residual power over you. This chapter explores ways to do so through an internal voyage of self-discovery. The healing methods listed here helped me to break unwanted ties to the past and open doors to a future full of possibilities.

After leaving an abusive relationship, a new location or job represents a new physical beginning. However, simply changing your physical surroundings won't result in healthy relationships and life choices if you're still carrying around the same old self-deprecating thoughts. The methods I've described in this chapter can override old false beliefs and promote the formation of new thoughts that represent the truth of who you are. To explore your internal depth and unearth your true self takes time, just as it took time for your abuser to destroy your sense of self-confidence. However, the process is worth every minute. How you feel about yourself is paramount to the quality of your life. As we regain our power, everything around us shifts to align with our new perceptions and expectations.

As mentioned earlier, this sort of exploration is likely to unearth difficult memories and feelings, so it's important to have the help of good friends who will be there when you need to talk and encourage you to keep going. I spent lots of time talking with a friend who was going through her own healing process. We encouraged each other to continue and suggested ways to get through some of the more difficult issues. Our time together was and still is invaluable.

Counseling: When I finally realized I needed professional help, I sought out a female psychologist. Although she was somewhat helpful in revealing how my background had influenced my choices, she was not trained in domestic violence and thus did not have the specialized education to properly assist me. I highly recommend professional help, but I encourage you to search out only those who specialize in domestic abuse. You can start by calling the HOTLINE or checking with your local shelter. Shelters in your area will normally provide free counseling services and/or be able to recommend someone with the appropriate experience and training.

Your counselor might also recommend seminars, books, or other resources to foster your healing.

New Age thought – spirituality: For me, the breakthrough to finding trust in myself, taking back my power, and truly gaining self-esteem for the first time in my life came through New Age spiritual teachings, support, and study. Spiritual (not religious) philosophies have a major focus on the beauty of each individual. They offer a positive way of thinking without dogma, guilt, and/ or judgment getting in the way. This unlimited outlook on life encourages all people to see their value and gain the courage to live fearlessly, helping others along the way.

My introduction to the New Age thought process began with reading and listening to books by New Age authors such as Wayne Dyer, Brené Brown, Louise Hay, Neale Donald Walsch, Gary

Zukav, Byron Katie, Mike Dooley, Marianne Williamson, and Michael Beckwith. New Age thinking is actually 200 years old and was practiced by individuals such as Ralph Waldo Emerson and Henry David Thoreau.

New Age thought includes uncovering the unconscious false thoughts about ourselves and various aspects of our lives, discovering the origin of these thoughts, and replacing them with the truth. This process is incredibly important, because a new beginning won't help much if we continue to harbor the same old self-effacing thoughts. I learned this lesson the hard way, initially repeating many bad choices after I left my abuser. I continued to do so until I reached out for help.

In time I discovered my local Center for Spiritual Living. Being around like-minded, caring people was instrumental in learning to value and trust myself.

Choose whatever methods foster your true internal power, with power defined simply as self-confidence and self-esteem, deeply rooted in love for yourself. This definition is not meant to imply arrogance or selfishness in any way. Love of self is the basis for healthy, loving relationships. We can only give what we have. To that end, loving oneself is the basis for all love we give and all love that enters our lives.

True thoughts – reprogramming the brain: We have control over our minds. We have the ability to observe our thoughts and we can govern what and how we think. As the Buddha put it: *Mind is a beautiful servant, but a dangerous master.*

Once I began to observe my self-deprecating thoughts, I was able to list them and their origin, describe why they were false, and replace them with the truth. For example, let's say your abuser instilled in you a deep-seated belief that you are selfish. List that thought, where it came from, and why this belief is not true.

121

Think about how you care for others, your generosity, and anything you do or desire to do that helps people, animals, and/or the earth. In reality, your abuser was the selfish one, and any description he gave you was strictly designed to systematically destroy your sense of self. The truth of who you are has nothing to do with his or anyone else's assessment of you. Next time the thought "I am selfish" pops into your head, replace it with something like "I am a caring person." I found this exercise to be quite useful.

Although you can't just flip a switch and make the old thoughts go away, by recognizing such thoughts as they come up and replacing them with the truth, it is possible to slowly but surely reprogram your brain. Repetition is what ingrained these old, false thoughts into your consciousness in the first place, and repetition is what can replace them with new thoughts that are true. What we think of ourselves has quite an influence over who we attract into our lives, what paths open for us, what choices we make, and the amount of love that surrounds us.

Courage – stepping outside your comfort zone: Letting go of old beliefs takes courage, but courage begets courage. When I escaped from my abuser, I was afraid of everything and had to begin to face my fears one small step at a time. The more we take even the smallest steps outside our comfort zone, the more our courage grows. Remember that you have already done one of the most, if not the most courageous thing in your life: You left your abuser. You are tremendously courageous already.

The following list contains more examples of courageous acts. Because the items on this list may seem small at face value, you may not have considered them in this way.

- Speaking up for yourself
- Attending a class by yourself

- Going out to eat or to a movie by yourself

- Going on an adventure by yourself

- Defining and setting your boundaries (see *Chapter 19* for a list of basic relationship rights)

- Asking for help

- Navigating a difficult conversation, establishing the requirements for all to come to the table with respect and kindness and the desire to understand versus defend—*no interrupting allowed*

- Joining a group and meeting new friends. One way to meet like-minded people is to search for a Meetup Group that interests you. (Google *Meetup Groups* to find groups near you.)

Loving yourself: This exercise points out the foundational necessity of loving yourself before you can truly love others. That's a strange concept to most of us. I had never consciously felt love for myself until one day, a few weeks after I'd finished a three-month-long process of overcoming deep mental wounds, I decided to take a walk.

As I was walking, I started to think about how it feels to love another or a pet and then consciously turned those feelings toward myself. What an amazing experience. I realized this was the first time I'd ever had loving and appreciative thoughts toward myself. It's quite an epiphany to realize that you've rarely if ever thought about yourself in positive terms. Try this exercise after you've spent time getting to the truth of who you are.

Listing your positive attributes: The goal of this exercise is to focus on your good qualities. Have you ever thought about what makes you wonderful? That's a foreign idea for many of us. Start the list, maybe on your phone, and add to it as you recognize more of your positive qualities. Refer to it when you need a boost of reality. Some ideas include acknowledging that you are kind, caring, intelligent, good to animals, a loving parent, organized, a good friend, helpful, generous, and/or resourceful.

Journaling: As mentioned earlier, journaling is an effective way to get thoughts out of your head and onto paper, which definitely reduces stress. I love journaling for that reason, but what amazes me almost as much is the mental clarity it uncovers. When I'm dealing with a problem, I'm no longer surprised to find the answer showing up as I'm writing about it.

Meditation: Meditation can help you focus and connect to your true self. It can also decrease blood pressure, reduce stress, and enhance concentration. Don't get all balled up in what some say are meditation "rules," like sitting cross-legged with your hands resting on your knees, palms up. Mediation works in whatever position is comfortable for you.

Most meditation begins with several deep breaths. Why? Does something happen in the body that causes us to relax when we breathe deeply? The answer is yes. When we expand our lungs, we stimulate the vagus nerve. This stimulation activates the parasympathetic nervous system, which prompts rest, relaxation, and good digestion. In other words, the parasympathetic nervous system mitigates the impact of stress on our bodies.

Once you have taken several deep breaths and begun to feel the results, it's time to begin your meditation. Sit quietly, breathe regularly, and concentrate on your breathing. Thoughts will come and go. That's normal. If a thought comes to mind, just let it pass, watch it float away, and return to focused breathing. Sometimes it may feel as if you are being bombarded with disorderly thoughts from every direction, and your mind wants to race. That's okay. Over time, meditation will help quiet your mind. You may discover that your quiet mind has great strength and power. It can reject thoughts that do not serve you and invite thoughts that are supportive, creative, and positive. Like anything else, meditation improves with practice. You also can pose a question to the Universe as part of your meditation and see what answers may show up. (Sometimes an answer will come to you and sometimes it won't.)

I'm not one to sit still for very long, so I prefer to meditate on nature walks, focusing on my steps, my breathing, and the surrounding beauty. Meditation is all about quieting extraneous thoughts to make room for creative thoughts to come in and answers to rise to the top of your consciousness. Howsoever you structure the process to work for you is fine.

Some people prefer guided meditations, where a soothing voice walks you through the meditation process. If you think this approach is something you would enjoy, check out the many free meditation apps and YouTube videos available for your smartphone and other devices.

Watching documentaries on unconscious conditioning: The documentaries *Miss Representation* and *The Mask You Live In* reveal the many ways the human brain is socially and culturally infected with false beliefs.[17] Google "The Representation Project" to watch the trailers for these films, find out where they are streaming, or purchase a copy.

Eliminating self-deprecating beliefs left from childhood: More than ten years ago, psychologist Leon F. Seltzer, PhD, wrote, "The very essence of our evolution depends on our ability to access, make peace with, and then fully integrate that insecure, self-doubting child that has constrained us in our lifelong journey toward self-actualization."[18] I have found this statement to be 100 percent true.

The beliefs we absorb during childhood can play a direct role in our acceptance of abuse. As Dr. Seltzer explains, the remedy for dealing with these damaging feelings:

> . . . has mostly to do with coming into our own authority as adults. We need to realize that whatever feelings of insecurity may still bother us probably have a lot less to do with the facts of our adult existence than the self-doubts best viewed as "holdovers" (or remnants) from childhood.[19]

After reading Dr. Seltzer's article, I adopted his recommendations to help me reconcile the deepest wounds from my past. Although I had successfully worked on many other issues over the years in a variety of ways, the most stubborn and deeply ingrained were the ones I addressed through this process.

As Dr. Seltzer explained, one way "....to facilitate the child's getting over these original feelings of fear, inadequacy, or powerlessness—is through undertaking some sort of internal dialogue."[20] Following is an explanation of the steps I took to engage in that inner dialogue as I addressed each issue on my list. Over a period of approximately three months, the disciplined approach of working most days for an hour or more proved life-changing.

As I addressed my issues mentally, I also wrote down my thoughts and feelings. So often survivors, myself included, have had their experiences denied, trivialized, or distorted. Writing brought clarity by providing the opportunity to define my own reality and culminated in a permanent record of my healing progress.

I'm not saying this approach dissolved each of my concerns immediately or completely—for some concerns it did, for others it did not. However, as you read through the steps, you'll see how the last step provides a way to deal with any concerns that are not fully resolved.

As you follow each step, you will be working with an inner partner, your "child-self," or the person you were as a child. Together, the two of you will review what happened in your past, how it influenced you, and how it made you feel. Providing both the child you were and the adult you are now with adult interpretations of past events will help the little girl within you realize she is now all grown up.

For me, the best way to begin this process was to go back in time, as early as I could, and list every triggering issue/experience from childhood I could recall. Then, for each item I listed, I adapted Dr. Seltzer's advice as I:

- Asked my child-self how she interpreted the event and what it made her think about herself For example: not good enough, not smart enough, not pretty enough.

- Talked to my upset child-self. I imagined holding her. I explained to her that's she's now grown up, a part of the competent adult who's returned to rescue and help her as we work together to revise old, false, out-of-date views of ourselves.

- Looked through pictures of myself when I was growing up and shared some of them with my child-self. These visual reminders helped me see the caring adult I became.

- Finally, I gave my child-self fresh data to help invalidate the negative thoughts she's carried about herself all these years. I talked to my child-self about each event, sometimes explaining why it was unfair, sometimes discussing the person(s) who caused it and why they were out of line (adults make mistakes, too), and then providing the truth about how she can perceive the situation as a grownup.

According to Dr. Seltzer, "Giving the child fresh data to help invalidate the negative image they formed about themselves so many years ago will help upgrade their sense of self like nothing else."[21]

I can second that, but if you take this road, *don't stop there*! Continue the journey by writing about the positive lesson(s) and anticipated lifelong effect(s) or benefit(s) of having dealt with each issue/experience. Then explain these results and benefits to your child-self. With any experience, good or bad, comes wisdom. As you can imagine, discerning that wisdom (positive lesson[s] and lifelong effect[s]) can require some pondering. I sometimes had to walk away from the process for a time because I couldn't imagine any positive effect resulting from some of the stuff I lived through, but the answers eventually came to me.

The beauty and importance of these lessons/benefits is that they give you a different way to perceive each issue you address. For example, should an old tape start to play in your head regarding an issue that has not been completely resolved, you can immediately override it by focusing on the lifelong changes and positive lessons provided by the issue. Eventually, I believe this method will result in untethering from the event, as it did for me.

If you are dealing with a deep-seated lack of self-worth that began in childhood, I encourage you to give this method a try. No one needs to know what you're doing or why. I kept the process to myself until a few months after I completed it and could feel the tremendous healing that had taken place. I felt lighter, brighter, and released from the past. At that point, it was time to begin sharing it with others who needed help.

Positive lessons and lifelong effects: As you are recording your positive lessons/lifelong effects, you may want to write or type them in a different color so you can easily refer back to them as needed. Here are examples of lessons learned/effects realized from the difficult times in my life:

- Perseverance, respect for money, determination to stay fit and trim, independence, the ability to fend for myself

- Discernment, hypervigilance, courage

- An understanding of where my responsibilities end and another's begin

- How to put myself first in instances where I otherwise would have thrown myself under the bus for someone else

- The importance of defining and defending my boundaries

- The realization that I gave my power away to men and the knowledge of how to cease doing so and remain in my power

- An understanding of my need to research and discover what a good marriage actually looks and feels like

- How to define the type of life partner I am looking for and the willingness to settle for nothing less

- The realization that I need only let people into my life with whom I share an abundance of mutual support, respect, and appreciation

Cutting the cord to old relationships: I also applied this process to my abusive marriage, because during that part of my life I was operating from a wounded child's perspective—mainly from a lack of self-worth. I wrote from the standpoint of the mistreatment I was willing to accept from my abuser based on a lack of self-esteem generated by my childhood experiences. I talked to my child-self, showing her how we grew in courage, knowledge, and self-worth as we dumped the abuser and moved on.

At the very end of this long inner journey, it became clear that I'd spent my life viewing myself through the unfiltered eyes of a little girl who truly believed she was an inferior person. Until then, I never had taken the time to focus on the truth of who I was. I wondered what it would feel like if the thoughts I had about myself were positive, kind, and caring. I really didn't know. To answer this question, I wrote a list of positive attributes that I now could see were accurate. If you haven't done so already, you may wish to create your own list of positive attributes. It's very helpful to review when feelings of insecurity arise.

⊷⊶

As you explore various aspects of the healing process, it's important to remember that how you dress, how you look, what you know, your dreams, your likes and dislikes, your career—everything that makes you who you are—are all okay. You don't have to be like anyone else or try to become like a person someone else prefers. There is no one else on this earth like you. Take pride in who you are. Rise in your own dignity.

It took me many years to feel good in my own skin, but it was a wonderful journey. I hope that sharing what I learned through trial and error will help make your journey smoother and significantly shorten your healing process.

Live from your strength.
Trust in yourself.
Refuse to receive anyone's condemnation.

Chapter 13

Life Changes When We Rediscover Ourselves

*"Resolve to be thyself, and know that they who find
themselves, lose their misery."*
—Matthew Arnold[22]

*L*ife definitely changes when we begin to see ourselves as valuable, loving, worthy, courageous, intelligent, and capable women. But what does it mean to view ourselves in such a positive light? How does this change in mindset make a difference in our everyday lives?

This list highlights what I learned to focus on as I reclaimed myself and acknowledged my self-worth. Your list might look different than mine, but I wager several of these items would show up on both.

- **Understand and forgive the old me for past choices:** As we grow, learn, and change, it's so easy to look back and beat ourselves up for getting into an abusive relationship in the first place and/or for not leaving sooner. Recognizing that we were doing the best we could with what we knew and who we were at the time helps us forgive ourselves and focus instead on the massive amount of courage it took to get out.

- **Untether myself from those who harmed me:** Without excusing the behavior of our abuser(s), we can free ourselves from the bitterness that tied us to them.

- **Realize I am worthy of love just as I am:** We don't have to be perfect to be lovable. No one is perfect, but everyone is worthy of love. We are enough just as we are.

- **Connect with people on a much deeper level:** Learning to love ourselves can result in an astonishing opening of the heart toward others.

- **Make many new friends and reconnect with old ones.**

- **Step outside my comfort zone:** As our courage increases, we often find ourselves eager to experience new things.

- **Dream again:** Planning for the future, making career choices, going back to school, forming new relationships, undertaking creative projects, learning and experiencing new places or activities, and so much more are part of awakening to who we are and our new freedoms. When our main focus is survival, we have no room to dream.

- **Enjoy creative thinking again:** We had to leave our wants and needs behind in order to maneuver inside an abusive relationship. When our creative thoughts start to flow, it's so empowering. Anything from making a new recipe, solving a problem, fixing something that is broken, decorating, crafting, and more builds our confidence and makes us aware of our abilities. Believe it or not, it's the little things that make for an extraordinarily enjoyable life.

- **Fill my calendar with plans:** Scheduling a variety of activities with a variety of people provides opportunities to explore a world that was closed to us for so long.

- **Help others:** As opportunities arise, we can lend our time, talents, and/or financial support to organizations that interest us.

- **Travel and go on adventures by myself:** Lone travel, across town to a restaurant or across the country, is something many people fear, even those who have never been in abusive relationships. In my case, the thought of traveling alone was initially inconceivable, but now it's exciting. Courage increases over time.

- **Rediscover what gives me joy and pursue those things:** Being able to think about what adventures or activities we enjoy and take part in them again is so much fun. We had to give up fun; it's fantastic to get it back.

- **Become very discerning about the people I let into my life:** We can choose to accept only those with whom we can share mutual support. We've experienced the worst; now it's time to choose people who meet our criteria for healthy interactions.

- **Realize the characteristics of a good partner and a good relationship:** See *Chapter 14* for information about choosing a life partner and *Chapter 16* for information about healthy relationships. Healthy relationships, romantic or otherwise, are the only kind worth pursuing or accepting. *Never compromise!*

- **Appreciate that marriage is a choice:** Some of us may marry again or live with another in a long-term relationship; others may remain single. Some may prefer a relationship structure often labeled as LAT (Living Apart Together), where a dedicated couple, married or not, chooses to maintain separate households. Any choice we make going forward is fine, as long as it *is* a choice. Nowhere is it written in stone that marriage is a requirement for happiness.

- **Thoroughly enjoy my own company:** We all need a different mix of social and alone time, but sometimes nothing beats nesting in your own strength and doing whatever you want.

- **Trust myself, my intelligence, and my choices:** All our lives we've been told what to believe, and our abuser wanted us to believe we were totally incompetent. As we heal, we learn to *think for ourselves*. What an incredible feeling of freedom! What we believe is what resonates in our hearts. Self-referencing allows us to choose from a broad range of options in making life choices and helps us to avoid relying on traditional authorities or the belief systems of others.

- **Feel the exhilaration of freedom:** Freedom is so precious. It creates its own overwhelming love of life, along with a sense of perpetual gratitude.

- **Feel completely comfortable in my own skin:** Healing brings an inner sense of security and independence. We know that we are enough and we know that we matter. Be proud of who you are.

- **Put an end to body shaming:** Society says a woman's body is terribly inadequate unless it meets some bizarre definition of perfection. The advertising industry is focused on getting us to buy into this myth, but the whole premise is totally nuts. Our bodies are amazing and miraculous. Our bodies have kept us going all our lives. So what's not to love? We can honor our bodies by focusing on keeping them healthy, by choosing nutritious food, and by remaining active. We can further honor ourselves by consciously dismissing ridiculous, unobtainable notions of physical perfection. It's not about how society says we should look; it's about what works for us.

Chapter 14

Choosing a Life Partner

*"What greater thing is there for two human souls than to
feel that they are joined... to strengthen each other... to be
at one with each other in silent unspeakable memories."*

—George Eliot

*N*ow that you've spent the time and done the work to
rediscover who you are, untether yourself from the past, know
your basic human rights, and set your boundaries, how does it feel
to be able to stand in your power? It's an amazing, life-changing
transformation, isn't it? Internal work allows us to avoid repeating
the same damaging relationship choices, as well as to bond with
another without losing ourselves. We're all hardwired to want
companionship, but before jumping into the dating pool, take the
time to list the characteristics you're looking for in a partner. This
might be the first time you've ever made such a list.

My goal in this chapter is to help you set your relationship bar at
its highest point. Without this information, it's very easy to choose
a man who, while better than the abuser of your past, is still not
a good man. Say, for instance, you meet a man who is funny,
generous, and makes a good living; who listens when you speak
and loves to cook; who would never physically hurt you. Seems
like a huge and fabulous improvement over living sequestered with
someone whose goal is to destroy you mentally, physically, and
emotionally. However, this new man also proves to be publicly
demeaning, unable to communicate, passive-aggressive, and a
chronic liar. One would not necessarily label such a man abusive,

but it's a safe bet to say his relationship skills leave much to be desired.

Over time, if this man is unable or unwilling to acknowledge his unhealthy relationship skills and replace them with healthy ones, he may end up abusing his partner emotionally, mentally, and verbally, because that's all he knows. If you set your relationship bar at the top, you will not find yourself in this situation because you will accept nothing less than a good man.

Have you ever consciously considered that *choosing a life partner is one of the most important decisions you can make as the predictor of your future happiness or misery?* Professor, author, and podcast host Brené Brown, PhD, defines connection as "The energy that exists between people when they feel seen, heard, and valued; when they can give and receive without judgment; and when they derive sustenance and strength from the relationship."

When you look back on the men you've allowed into your life, did you just roll with the punches without much focus on the core attributes you preferred in a partner? I certainly did. When I married my ex, I didn't know anything about his financial situation, political beliefs, preferences regarding children, religious ideals, communication skills or lack thereof, man/woman-relationship role definitions, or what he felt about handling money within a relationship. I didn't know enough to even consider the issues outlined in this chapter. Only later did I realize I had chosen someone who not only would contribute nothing to the marriage but who would embark on a path to slowly and deliberately destroy me, inside and out.

We're not taught about relationships in our society, which is why so many people jump blindly into marriage unprepared. Can you picture how differently we would approach choosing a partner if both genders received relationship education beginning at a young age? Imagine how many marriages would be saved from divorce.

One of the benefits that can come from living through hard relationships is the acquisition of discernment and hypervigilance regarding who you will and will not let stand in the foyer of your life. The idea is to first determine what core values you must see in a potential partner and to then consider only those men who exhibit these values, regardless of what your hormones tell you. It's easy and quite common to be swept away by passion, only to have the relationship not work out due to a lack of compatibility. In other words, just because you are physically attracted to a man *doesn't mean he is a good choice for you.* Our society incorrectly encourages selecting a partner based solely on emotion when, in reality, the most successful long-term partner choices are made with a combination of logic and emotion. Of course, those things that initially draw us together—physical, spiritual, and mental attraction—are important, but equally important are issues of compatibility. Determining whether these harmonious connections truly exist between the two of you requires conscious effort, frequent and in-depth communication, and observation.

Compatibility is part of the foundation of a long-lasting relationship. When a couple is compatible, communication, sex, and daily living flow easily the majority of the time. We've all heard that relationships are hard work. When a couple is compatible, they may not agree with that statement. That's not to say life is trouble-free, but when the couple has problems, they normally can work them out. Compatible people mostly live together in harmony because they're usually on the same page. Members of a well-matched couple do not have to be clones of one another. That would be rather boring. More often than not, however, having a lot in common helps a couple continue to feel in love with each other versus constantly butting heads when their core values, daily living preferences, sexual needs, financial strategies, family values and expectations, child-rearing ideas, and/or work ethics inevitably come into conflict. The book *Will Our Love Last?* by Sam R. Hamburg, PhD, provides a thorough education on how to evaluate a compatible partner.

If and when you feel ready to consider allowing another to enter your life, here are some of the compatibility traits that support a healthy, long-lasting relationship.

Humor: Sharing a similar sense of humor is paramount in a good relationship. Humor helps us navigate hard times and make the most of not-so-enjoyable situations like airport delays, long lines, or dealing with things that break around the house. Being able to approach such issues with humor and not sweat the small stuff is a wonderful quality in a long-term relationship. Couples that have fun together share a beautiful connection.

Good communication skills: The majority of us have never been taught good communication skills, yet effective communication is fundamental to a healthy long-term relationship. It's important to find a partner who shares your desire to work through any issues that arise in a respectful way, someone with whom you feel safe discussing anything. When two people approach a difficult conversation with the desire to understand rather than defend, they are off to a very good start. This means waiting until both partners are calm and ready to listen. Good communication is worth its weight in gold.

It's also important that both parties enjoy talking with each other, not just about important issues but also in an exchange of casual conversation about daily happenings. If a couple is not on the same page in this area, the one who enjoys conversation might begin to feel lonely. To me, having an easy flow of daily communication ranging from the benign to the silly to the in-depth and serious is necessary to feel continually connected to the other person. It's one of the main activities that breathes life into a relationship.

A very wise woman once said, "Choose someone you can talk to. You can't stay in bed forever."

Being interested in discussing the compatibility between the two of you is also necessary. Have you ever considered sitting down with a good potential partner to determine each of your views on raising children, finances, sexual preferences, home upkeep, family traditions, religion and politics, and anything else important to either of you? This level of frank discourse should be a given before a couple moves into a dedicated relationship, but in our society, such discussions are rarely even mentioned, let alone encouraged.

For help with communication skills, consider reading the book *Why Marriages Succeed or Fail: And How You Can Make Yours Last* by John Mordecai Gottman. An American psychologist and professor emeritus of psychology at the University of Washington, Gottman has worked for over four decades on divorce prediction and marital stability. In his book, he uses a biblical metaphor, the Four Horsemen of the Apocalypse, to identify the four elements most likely to destroy a marriage: criticism, contempt, defensiveness, and stonewalling.

- Criticism: Attacking a partner at the core of his or her being.

- Contempt: Making a partner feel inept, worthless, and unloved using methods such as mocking them with sarcasm, ridicule, and/or name-calling.

- Defensiveness: Addressing a partner's area of concern by reversing blame onto the partner or changing the subject to the partner's "bad" behavior.

- Stonewalling: Withdrawing from the interaction, shutting down, or refusing to respond at all.

If there were Five Horsemen of the Apocalypse, I'd add deceit, since lying is also deadly to a marriage. Needless to say, none of these horsemen are part of a good relationship.

Trustworthiness and honesty: Without honesty, there can be no trust. Without trust, respect is nonexistent. Without respect, a true relationship does not exist.

Have you ever felt you could confide in the man who was supposed to love you? If you did confide in him, were you confident he wouldn't use your secrets against you or voice them in public? Could you rely on him not to lie to you? Were you certain he was not cheating on you? With my ex, I had to answer a resounding NO to every one of these questions.

How can you be sure the man you're considering is trustworthy? I wish I could provide a method that would answer this question with 100 percent accuracy, but I don't think such a method exists. All I can tell you is this. First, do your Internet research to confirm, as best you can, the integrity of his statements. (For information on how to do so, see *Chapter 20 – How to Investigate a Potential Partner.*)

Even if your research doesn't turn up any areas of concern, you still need to listen to your gut. Learn to trust your intuition. If something doesn't feel right, don't ignore it. If you feel he is worth getting to know, take your time in doing so. Be aware of the early-warning red flags listed in *Chapter 1 – Recognizing the Early-Warning Red Flags,* as well as some of the pitfalls common in the world of online dating as outlined in *Chapter 15 – Red Flags in Today's Dating World.* When things don't feel right, address them or move on as necessary.

Mutual respect: Many of us can only imagine coming home from work after a difficult day and feeling so safe and supported by our life partner that we want to sit down and tell him everything that happened. To have such respect for how he looks at life and how he gives us the gift of listening is life-affirming. To value his positive energy, knowing he'll allow us whatever space we need to vent and help us deal with the issue if asked, is a true gift.

Have there ever been any men in your life for whom you felt this kind of respect? When I faced that question squarely in my own life, I was surprised to realize the answer was an absolute *NO*, beginning with my father. A good relationship cannot exist without mutual respect, yet within so many relationships this kind of respect is sorely lacking.

Included in the category of mutual respect is the ability to see each other as equal partners. In a healthy relationship, there is a rotation of power. I think of it as handing the reins back and forth. Have you ever felt like the man in your life believed you could handle the reins as well as he? If the answer is no, I can definitely relate. However, as we work through the mental scars left from childhood and abusive relationships, we can gain that level of respect, along with similar levels of love and trust, towards ourselves. When we respect ourselves, no man will be allowed to enter our lives unless he views us as an equal and affords us that same level of respect. Male entitlement/dominance/ privilege is no longer allowed to exist in our world.

Common interests: Do you share an interest in similar activities, hobbies, adventures? Do you have similar preferences in friends? Imagine going out and doing things together on a regular basis and thoroughly enjoying the activity and each other's company. Of course, your interests won't overlap on everything, but having a good number of common interests is very important.

Compatible couples very often share a common passion. They have their "thing" such as dancing, kayaking, gardening, or writing. Many times couples who have been together for years and are still deeply in love will tell you they met while enjoying their common passion. Perhaps they were taking ballroom dancing lessons, attending a garden club meeting, or participating in a writing group.

Pursue whatever interests fuel *your* passion, and you'll meet like-minded people in the process.

Similar energy levels: It can be an issue if one person is in shape and active and the other is not, or if one person prefers a healthy menu and the other loves junk food. It may become very frustrating to be with someone who cannot keep up with you. Their lack of endurance can get in the way of your enjoyment of life. To me, it's important to be mostly on the same page when it comes to activities, exercise, and food preferences.

Curiosity: Have you ever found it difficult to carry on a conversation with certain people who just don't seem to hold up their end of the discussion? They could be shy, it's true, but it's also possible this lack of participation is due to a lack of curiosity. For example, if you mention to a potential partner that you are reading a book or taking a class, does the conversation end there, or does he ask about the book and/or the class? If no questions are forthcoming, it's not a good sign. I've found that a lack of curiosity can indicate a lack of interest in others, an inability to focus, or poor conversational skills. Curiosity bespeaks a variety of interests, facilitates good conversation, and contributes to an exciting, adventurous relationship. If he's not curious about what interests you in the beginning, he'll be even less so as time goes on.

Spiritual and political beliefs: I learned the hard way about the importance of being on the same page when it comes to these two topics. Differences here can be devastating to a relationship.

Kindness: Some people are just innately kind, good people. Kindness contributes to a strong foundation when both parties possess this core quality. Good people help others, pay attention to each other's needs and preferences, work to make a difference in the world, are there when needed, and are generally easygoing, fair, and forgiving.

Financial compatibility: Money is both a big relationship issue and one of the most common bones of contention between couples. Although money conversations might feel awkward, it is important not only to discuss each other's financial situation but to assure a potential partner's assertions are backed up by bank, savings, investment, and other appropriate statements. No one wants to enter a dedicated relationship with someone who is up to their eyeballs in debt. Do you both keep a good handle on your funds? Do you have similar spending habits? Do you have similar feelings about saving money on a regular basis? It's difficult when one person spends willy-nilly and the other is more frugal and a more committed money manager. Do you each agree on the importance of keeping joint and separate bank accounts and credit cards? Even if you share joint accounts, it is *extremely* important that you always maintain an independent bank account and credit card as well.

Maintaining a household: A neatnik and a slob can find it very difficult to live under the same roof. Do both of you wish to maintain a tidy, clean, and organized home and yard? How are you matched when it comes to taking care of the home, inside and out? Who will do the shopping or the cooking or the cleaning or the laundry? Will these things be mutual responsibilities or does he have more traditional beliefs, expecting you to do it all? Are you on the same page as far as accumulating things? We live in a society that pushes consumerism, the philosophy of "more is better." Some people have embraced extremely simple living; those at the opposite end of the spectrum are hoarders. Where does each of you fall on this continuum? Do you each assign pretty much the same level of importance to home repairs? Some people can let noncritical repairs go for weeks, months, or even years; others feel strongly about fixing things as soon as they break.

Another clue to a potential partner's homemaking priorities can come from observing the place where's he's living now. If his current home is cluttered, dirty, and/or disorganized, and this mode of living is completely unacceptable to you, take heed! The person comfortable with clutter is not going to change, and a relationship where one person must do all the work to maintain some semblance of order can be an ongoing source of discord.

Sexual compatibility: Although sex is another frequent cause of disharmony, this conflict can be significantly reduced between couples who feel a high level of attraction to one another and who also share a similar level of interest in making love (sex drive) and sexual style. When this dimension of the relationship is satisfying, the commitment to monogamy is more likely to be honored.

Core values and outlook on life: This element of compatibility is about being on the same page when it comes to life's deep, core issues. Friendship and in-depth conversations about the things that are important stem from this type of compatibility. Do you agree on the big questions: spiritual beliefs; interest in having children and if so, how many; the proper way to raise children; political principles; balance between family and work; marriage; living together before (or instead of) marriage; the importance of honesty, trust, and respect; and the advisability of old-fashioned versus contemporary family ideals, to name a few? Without a good measure of commonality regarding these core values, both partners can feel very lonely.

When you and your partner have similar tastes, goals, interests, core values, etc., each affirms these similarities in the other. This affirmation happens frequently and naturally; no one has to work at it. A relationship of mutual confirmation, encouragement, and support is joyful and long-lasting.

Introspection: Introspection is not a universal human characteristic, but it is one I find priceless. If a man can't admit when he's made a mistake and/or he's not interested in learning through self-evaluation in the interest of his own personal growth (not to mention the resulting benefit to the relationship), he's not someone I would choose. Two people who can sit down and discuss an issue, learn from it, and subsequently consider and review how they could do better, is a combination that's invaluable.

The moral of this story: Only by paying attention to what you *feel* (attraction) plus what you *think* (compatibility), can you truly find a satisfying long-term relationship. Enjoy that fabulous mutual emotional "high" of chemistry and attraction, but don't make any long-term commitments until the love drug PEA has worn off and both of you see the relationship as consciously compatible!

The goal is to choose a partner who makes us "better" when we are helping them and when they are helping us. In this way, couples enhance each other's lives, and each partner feels validated and happier because of the relationship. Anything less is not worth it.

If you'd like help with these and other talking points regarding compatibility, the book *Will Our Love Last?* by Sam R. Hamburg, PhD, is a marvelous resource. *I highly recommend it!* The clarity it provides is priceless.

⊱◈⊰

> *"Being deeply loved by someone gives you strength,*
> *while loving someone deeply gives your courage."*
>
> —Lao Tzu

Chapter 15

Red Flags in Today's Dating World

"You are in charge of who you let into your life.
Don't settle for less than you deserve!"

—T. Ann DeCarlo

*I*f you decide you're ready to date again, you may discover the process is very different from when you were dating in years past. With that in mind, I want to warn you about a few things.

Meeting someone online requires caution. If you then decide to meet in person, you're more vulnerable in that you really have no idea who this person is. You can learn a lot about him by doing an online background check as explained in *Chapter 20 – How to Investigate a Potential Partner*, but even when armed with this information, you're still at risk when meeting a stranger.

Be sure to get any man's full name, phone number, and address (or at least the part of town in which he lives), before you agree to meet him. You'll need this information for a background check. If he won't provide it, decline any further communication because he is definitely trying to hide something. He may be in a relationship, married, living in another state or city, or be using a fake profile as part of a scam. Of course, he may ask you to provide the same information. Do not. He can find your address via the Internet if he knows your last name or phone number. Keep everything but your first name to yourself until you know who you're dealing with. If he continues to push you for more information or gets upset because you won't provide it at this very early stage, move on. He is either clueless as to the vulnerability of women in our society or he has ulterior motives. Either way, he's not worth your time.

The following are some red flags to watch for:

He has money issues: Does he have the means to date? If he doesn't, he may say he really wants to spend time with you but you'll have to pay your own way due to his financial situation. Look down the road. This scenario is not conducive to an enjoyable life. Is he a tightwad? Does he have trouble being generous? Even those with plenty of money can be bizarrely stingy. He could also be up to his eyeballs in debt.

The following are signs that he's either dealing with lack of funds or has tightwad/generosity issues:

- He orders one meal and has the waiter split it between the two of you without asking your permission.

- He asks for separate checks.

- He chooses a really cheap restaurant, or he only asks you to go on walks or other free forms of entertainment.

A man dealing with a lack of funds may be looking for a woman to save him from his financial woes. Move on.

Does he pay with cash? Paying with cash can simply be a preference or it can be a red flag. Cash can't be traced. Paying with cash can mean he's declared bankruptcy and has relinquished his credit cards, or that he is married or in a relationship where he doesn't want to leave a credit card trail.

He is alone for a good reason: Has he been divorced for several years without any long-term relationships within that time? Examples: He tells you he's been divorced for ten years, but the longest relationship he's had during that time lasted only three weeks. Or, his two marriages were both very short in duration and he's been single for many years but claims to have been engaged twice within that timeframe. He says the engagements simply "didn't work out." Run! No doubt there's a good reason why he's alone and why his relationships/marriages didn't last long. There's also no good reason to find out why.

He can't be trusted: Has he lied about anything in his dating profile like height, where he's from, interests, or age? Anyone who is willing to lie in his profile may be willing to lie about much bigger things. As soon as you find out a man has lied, particularly about something important like his finances or marital status, head for the door. Do not give him a second chance. Accepting even the smallest of lies at this early stage teaches him you'll put up with it.

What particularly puzzles me is a man who lies either about where he is from and/or his height. It may be obvious as soon as you meet him that he lied about his height, which says he's not only a liar but he's not very bright. Some men will say they live in your area, but when you do a background check, the results show their current address is in a different city or state. I've seen this happen twice. One man was legitimately in the process of moving to the city listed in his profile but didn't bother to explain this discrepancy (his height was a lie as well). The real story about the other guy, who also lived in another state, was never discovered. A relationship can't work without trust.

He hides physical attributes: A man who doesn't smile in his dating profile pictures could be trying to look macho; he also could be hiding bad teeth. If his pictures only show him from the shoulders up, he may be trying to obscure a giant gut. If good teeth and a thin body are important to you, you may want to consider a video call before considering an in-person meeting.

He immediately begins asking for favors: Do not agree to any favors a man asks of you when he barely knows you. This is a sign that he could be a user and/or is looking for a mommy. We all have the right to ask anything of anyone; we also have the right to say no to any request. If a man asks you for a favor before you've met in person or even after your first couple of dates, ask yourself if you would feel comfortable asking *him* for a favor at this early stage of the relationship or if he would ever ask a man to do this same favor under similar circumstances. I've found this sort of favor-asking to be amazingly common. It's as though these men can't wait to delegate the mundane details of daily life to a woman. Needless to say, there's no equality in this scenario.

Here are a few examples of favors men have asked women in the early stages of a relationship. The answer in each case was *NO*—no to the favor and no to any future dates:

- Could she drive him to another city to pick up a car?

- Would she wash the new clothing he just bought?

- Could he bring his laundry to her house? (In one instance, a man showed up at the woman's house with his dirty laundry without even asking.)

- Could she review a letter he had written?

- Could she review his website copy?

- Could they become business partners because he wants to be part of her future plans?

- Would she help him with *his* new business plans?

- Would she please do the driving when they are together because he doesn't want to put miles on his leased car?

He appears to be using a fake profile: There are many fake profiles on dating sites. Some of the common giveaways are a profile that includes only one picture or consists of professional pictures that look like they came from stock photo sites; or a profile that indicates an advanced degree but the writing is inept and clumsy and/or contains grammatical or spelling errors. Other red flags: He has plenty of excuses as to why he can't meet and asks for favors or money to fix his car, pay his rent, cover medical bills, etc. Never agree to send money to anyone you meet on a dating site. It's *always* a scam. Another weird common thread in fake profiles is the frequent use of "LOL" within their messages or texts. These scammers can also be overly complimentary.

He doesn't care for his home: If you visit his home and it's a pig pen, pay attention, because his lack of interest in the cleanliness of his surroundings is not going to change. It has been my experience that a man who is incapable or uninterested in keeping up his home will be a burden, not a partner.

To keep yourself safe, it's best not to agree to get into a man's car unless you have done a background check and have spent enough time getting to know him that you feel confident that he is who he says he is. Of course, the same applies to going to his place, allowing him to know where you live, or visiting your home.

He has substance-abuse issues: Some men may have a substance-abuse problem and be trying to hide it. Beware if he exhibits a desire to smoke pot every chance he gets and perhaps mix it with alcohol. (For many people, smoking pot occasionally, like having the occasional drink, is not a problem. Chronic daily use, however, indicates someone who can't cope with life.) Does he have a large stash of one or the other or both? Watch how much he drinks when you're out on a date. Look at his eyes to see if he's stoned. Notice if you smell pot when he shows up for a date. Watch to see if he takes pills frequently without mentioning what they're for.

A man can only hide his addictions for so long, and the sooner you find out, the faster you can avoid wasting any more time on the guy.

He wants to remain friends: Once you've determined you are not interested in pursuing a relationship with a man but he asks if you can remain friends, ask for his definition of friendship. This situation can be a setup. If his definition involves continuing to go out as though you are a couple and/or communicating every day, deny the request or explain your boundaries for friendship.

In my experience, it is common for a man to believe that if he can get you to agree to stay in touch and spend a lot of time together "as friends," he'll eventually be able to persuade you to become a couple. Bottom line: He's not hearing you and is only interested in what he wants. You have said no to becoming a couple, but he sees this answer as negotiable.

There's no reason to waste your time with a man who does not interest you, hear you, or respect your wishes. Move on. Do what is best for you. If he gets mad because of your lack of interest or won't take no for an answer—continues to ask you out, text you, etc.—block him on your phone, email, dating sites, and social media.

I've seen this remain-friends setup play out badly several times. It's one reason I encourage you to keep your address to yourself, giving it out only when you are satisfied the man who interests you is trustworthy. The last thing you need is an upset nutcase of a man showing up at your door.

> *"If you cannot find a good companion to walk with, walk alone,*
> *like an elephant roaming the jungle. It is better to be alone*
> *than to be with those who will hinder your progress."*
>
> —the Buddha

Just as there are red flags to help us identify men who would not make good partners, there are plenty of other indicators, "green flags" if you will, that make potential relationships worth pursuing.

He pursues you: He is interested and focused on getting to know you and mature enough to know how to treat you. If you have indicated you are not interested and he continues to pursue, this characteristic becomes a red flag.

He plans dates: He listens to what you like, takes the reins, and makes it happen. He does the research as to location, operating hours, etc., and asks you to join him on the adventure he has planned with your tastes in mind.

The opposite of this sort of consideration is sticking you with making all the plans and decisions. As an example, one man I had just started dating called to ask if I'd like to visit a particular historical site. At the time I was sick in bed with a cold but said I'd love to when I was feeling better. His response was to ask me to do the computer research to find out everything we needed to know about the place *he'd* suggested we visit. That was the end of him.

He's focused and courteous during conversations: He looks at you and listens when you speak. His phone is off or at least on vibrate when you're together. When the two of you are talking, in person or on the phone, he's not doing anything that takes his attention away from the conversation.

One time I was on the phone with a man when I noticed he seemed a bit distracted. We had already gone out a few times, so I asked why, and he said he was trying to catch up on reading his emails. Another man showed his lack of communication and listening skills on the first date. He asked me a question and then spent his time looking around the restaurant while I answered. Neither of these men was worth more of my time.

He does as much for you as you do for him: He recognizes the need for equality in a good relationship. He knows your worth and makes sure you recognize it, too. He's not looking for a pat on the back or brownie points because he's good to you. He treats you well because he loves seeing a smile on your face.

He loves you every day: He sees your value and shows it through appreciation of all the little things you do. You feel loved as opposed to taken for granted. His default mode is kindness and consideration. He puts an effort into keeping you and making you happy.

When making love, he gives as often as he receives.

☙❦❧

Finding a good man to whom you are attracted and with whom you are compatible (see *Chapter 14 – Choosing a Life Partne*r) can take time and patience. There is no hurry. Let the process unfold in its own time. In the meantime, single life has many wonderful perks. Enjoy them!

Chapter 16

Characteristics of a Healthy Relationship

"A healthy relationship is a feast of affection/giving for both people;
not one receiving crumbs and trying to convince themselves it's enough."
—Shannon Thomas

Chapter 14 focused on some of the areas to consider when choosing a life partner, recognizing that this choice can be a life-altering decision. Now that you've taken the time to describe the characteristics of a partner you're willing to let into your life, let's look at how this internal hard work, combined with your choice of a good man, can result in an enjoyable, long-lasting union.

Have you ever witnessed a healthy marriage? "No" is a very common answer. Most of us begin by basing our relationship standards on what we saw and experienced growing up, since this dynamic is what we're most familiar with. When our parents had anything but a healthy relationship, it's common for us to have low expectations for the well-being of our own relationships, albeit often unintentionally. It's not as if we've been encouraged to sit down with a promising potential partner and discuss each other's description of a healthy relationship. So we go with what we know, or what we think we know.

Healthy relationships begin with two people who are compatible and who can't imagine entering into a long-term commitment unless it is based on respect, honesty, fairness, negotiation, trust, kindness, integrity, and support. There is a give and take in a healthy partnership; both partners feel in control of their own personal actions and decisions. Both partners know they have the right to make their own choices about their respective lives.

When you're in a relationship that offers a safe and loving space to be who you are and to speak your mind, the groundwork is in place for the formation of healthy habits like the ones described below.

Speaking up when something is bothering you: Have you ever felt safe enough or loved enough to sit down with your partner and talk about something in the relationship or something he did that is not sitting right with you? Can you imagine your partner taking your hands and saying, "Don't worry, we'll get through this together"? With two committed people who love and respect each other, it's normal to have the desire, dedication, and patience to work things out. This mindset makes it possible to confront the situation with kindness, caring, and respect. Remember, it's okay to agree to disagree.

You don't have to talk about a potentially contentious issue immediately after it happens. Take whatever time you need to think about it and to be in a calm frame of mind when you bring it up. If you don't speak up, there is no way for your partner to learn from the experience, apologize, or adjust his behavior. If your partner cannot speak up in an equally respectful manner, there is no way for you to learn either. No relationship is without fault on either side. Conversely, no relationship can remain healthy without communication and vulnerability on both sides.

Being able to communicate with your partner about anything is crucial. Without this foundational pillar, everything eventually crumbles.

Being (and having) a partner willing to compromise: Neither person should be expected to throw his or her needs and desires under the bus for the other, but when both partners are willing to negotiate and compromise as needed, the results can be greater than either of them might have achieved alone.

Being honest about your feelings: In a good relationship, both people are safe to tell the truth and to be honest about how they feel. It's okay for both to be human and imperfect, and to be forgiven, loved, supported, and respected in spite of their imperfections. This kind of acceptance includes being able to discuss how you feel about an issue even when your partner feels differently.

Respecting each other's privacy and interests: We all need our alone time. It's wonderful to feel free to go off on our own with friends, work on our interests and hobbies, attend events that aren't of interest to our partner, and basically come and go as we please.

Deciding together: A healthy relationship is one based on equality. Couples in such a relationship make decisions together regarding major purchases, sexual needs, vacations, and parameters of money management. They look for ways to assure that both parties get their needs met.

Supporting and affirming each other: You have pride and respect for one another. You accept each other for who you are. You support each other's accomplishments, ideas, goals, successes, and desires. You each affirm characteristics in the other such as intelligence, creativity, integrity, and kindness. Having someone who believes in us makes it all that much easier to believe in ourselves and in our ability to meet our obligations and fulfill our dreams.

Taking responsibility for choices and actions: We all make mistakes, but living with someone who will not take responsibility for their words, actions, or choices is beyond frustrating. In a healthy relationship, both partners are mature enough to own what they did, apologize, learn from their mistakes, and move forward. The overall atmosphere of the relationship is one of security, love, and understanding, a safety net of respect, supported by trust, and designed to perpetuate open communication.

Spending time together: Being together is a joy. You want to spend time with each other doing anything from mundane chores around the house, grocery shopping, or volunteering, to setting off on exciting adventures. You make each other laugh and have a wonderful balance of togetherness and alone time.

Respecting personal boundaries: Partners in a healthy relationship recognize that each person is an individual whose boundaries and rights are worthy of respect. Unhealthy relationships are more like those of an owner and a slave. (See *Chapter 19 – Your Basic Human Relationship Rights* for more on this subject.)

⊸⊱⊰⊱⊰⊰⊰

Even the best relationships can be challenging at times, and all good relationships require energy and care. If you have trouble working through certain issues as a couple, you might consider getting help from a neutral third party. Sometimes talking with a counselor or therapist can help partners work through their problems and/or refine their communication skills in ways that significantly improve the relationship.

Nobody is perfect, but you can be imperfect together!

Section Three

Whether you are still living with your abuser, have recently left, or have made the transition and are building your new life, this last section may help you to better understand your own decisions as well as the life circumstances that formed the personality and subsequent behavior of your abuser. A separate chapter is devoted to the basic relationship rights to which every individual is entitled, and the final chapter provides a variety of references and resources you may find helpful.

Chapter 17

Why Do We Stay?

"The problem is, women think he will change; he won't.
And men make the mistake of thinking she will never leave; she will."

—Unknown

*I*t seems like such a no-brainer to outsiders. "Why don't abused women just leave?" they want to know. "What's the big deal?"

When the victim's friends or family ask these questions, they represent just one more criticism: "What's wrong with her that she can't get out?" or "Why did she stay so long?"

Without firsthand experience, it's very difficult for others to understand. It seems inconceivable to an outsider that anyone would put up with such horrible treatment. They don't get the extreme, insidious, manipulative, brain-changing, destructive nature of abuse and the constant fear it drapes over the victim. They also have lost sight of who the criminal is in these situations and instead assign blame to the injured party. This is one of the reasons why abused women eventually stop talking to their family and friends.

I've included this chapter for two very important reasons: (1) To remind you why you stayed as long as you did; and (2) To acknowledge and celebrate the courage it took to leave. I spent years beating myself up for not leaving sooner, wondering why I put up with his crap for so long. I don't want you to do the same.

At the same time, we are *always* responsible for our choices. We didn't understand then what we understand now. Once we knew better, we did better. We chose to escape. Don't beat yourself up for staying. Instead, pat yourself on the back for the guts it took to sever the relationship and take back your power.

Why does a woman stay in an abusive relationship? She stays for a variety of reasons. First and foremost is fear.

Fear for her life and fear of the unknown: The danger that exists in an abusive relationship is very real, and the level of danger can escalate significantly when a woman leaves. What will he do to her, to himself, to the children, or to pets?

Not only is she facing the unpredictable behavior of her partner, she also must face her own fears about creating a new life. How will she manage financially and socially? How will she handle being the sole provider for herself and her children? Will she face extreme loneliness? Is she loveable? The abuser may have drilled into her head that nobody else would ever have her. If she leaves, will she be alone for the rest of her life?

Remember, she is beginning this adventure from a state of extremely low self-esteem.

Believing she can make the abuse stop: Regardless of whether the woman is a strong career professional or a hardworking, stay-at-home mom, her sense of self can be destroyed by emotional abuse. Enduring a constant, daily bombardment of criticism can make almost any woman believe those messages eventually. The abuser is her judge and jury. His opinions of her rule her world. She believes that if she tries hard enough to become the person he wants, she can make the abuse stop. He has convinced her that she is responsible for all the problems in the relationship and that her actions are the reason he mistreats her.

The truth is, domestic abuse has *nothing* to do with the victim and everything to do with the demons in the abuser's head. Any woman would receive the same treatment at the hands of the abuser. He will never find any woman acceptable.

Never having experienced or witnessed a healthy relationship: This goes back to how we were raised. Some women don't know what a healthy relationship looks or feels like, so they accept an abusive relationship because it's all they have ever known. We humans gravitate toward the familiar. Familiarity has a stronger pull than comfort.

Women who experienced an abusive or otherwise psychologically unhealthy family dynamic growing up are more likely to experience poor self-esteem and have much lower partner/relationship expectations than women raised in a nurturing and supportive environment. Lacking the experience to identify healthy relationships, such women are vulnerable to becoming involved, often unknowingly, with an abuser who slowly traps them in his web.

Not realizing the abuser lacks the desire and relationship skills to change: The average person knows when they have behaved badly and/or hurt another and that some acknowledgment of that hurt, along with an apology, is appropriate for the well-being of both parties. The abuser will *never* apologize for his behavior.

All of us make mistakes. When we do, it's only natural to feel remorse and want to apologize, or at least not to do the same thing again. If someone has harmed us, we have every right to expect the same acknowledgment of remorse and apology in return. A man with a conscience will do his best to avoid repeating relationship mistakes. The abusive man's response, on the other hand, is pathological. Not only will he continue to replicate his abusive behavior but he won't even identify it as such. Even more troubling, the worst of abusers genuinely enjoy inflicting mental and physical pain.

As explained in *Chapter 5 – Why He Can't Change*, since an abuser sees nothing wrong with his behavior, *he is not a good candidate for rehabilitation*. Any form of his regret is manipulation in disguise, and his promises never to do it again can never be kept. He has one relationship skill and that is abuse. Expecting miraculous acquisition of healthy skills following a promise to change is expecting the impossible.

The abusive man is never going to wake up one morning and suddenly realize the error of his ways. Because an abused woman doesn't know this (or she doesn't believe it) she stays, hoping for normal behavior from a mentally compromised individual.

Needing to protect and/or fix the abuser: Along with expecting her abuser to miraculously change, a woman may feel guilty for betraying him. She believes he needs extra love and care because he has been wounded in the past. She feels it is her responsibility to help him become whole.

She is acting under the false assumption that he can change. Because she doesn't realize he is mentally ill, she thinks she can help him. No one can ever love an abuser into sanity or wholeness. Moreover, it is never anyone else's responsibility to make another person whole, nor is it possible. Internal change can only be accomplished by the individual.

Living with self-blame: The woman feels she is responsible for her abuser's behavior and/or that if she leaves, the resulting family breakup will be her fault. After all, he has told her over and over that she is the reason he gets upset, and because her self-esteem has been eliminated, she believes the lie.

She does not yet have the knowledge to understand that his behavior has nothing to do with her. He will find the same unreasonable faults with any woman. No woman can ever help him or be accepted by him.

Believing she must maintain her wedding vows: Abused women with strong religious beliefs can be tormented by how divorce is frowned upon by their religious tradition. However, in consulting with clergy, I have learned that no modern-day spiritual leader expects a woman to remain in an abusive relationship. After all, the abuser has already broken the vow he made to love and cherish his partner. No one can be in a partnership by themselves. "Till death do us part" does not apply when one partner has the potential to cause the death of the other.

Needing to believe all avenues for change have been exhausted: In researching the reasons why women stay in abusive relationships, I never came across this one. I'm including it, however, because it was one of the reasons I stayed, and I can't imagine I'm the only one who ever felt this way. I had to believe I had done everything in my power—tried everything I could think of—to make the relationship work before I threw in the towel. Little did I know that by continuing to stay I was both wasting my time and placing myself in ever-increasing danger.

Not realizing she has power: By subjecting his partner to unrelenting criticism, isolation, and emotional cruelty, the abuser destroys her self-esteem to the point where she feels completely powerless. Once he has her where he wants her, he continues to do whatever it takes to keep her trapped in his web.

In reality, the abuser needs the woman he is victimizing much more than she needs him. She is actually holding the cards, since having her abandon him is his worst fear.

Feeling shame and embarrassment: She doesn't want to tell anyone because it is embarrassing to admit she has allowed herself to get into or stay in this situation. She is ashamed of making poor decisions and of failing to make her marriage work.

In contrast, the truth is that she has been doing the best she can under unconscionable, no-win circumstances.

She denies the reality that the man she loves is capable of seriously hurting or killing her. Even though she knows he has hurt her in the past, she cannot believe he is truly an evil person because she would not have chosen to be with such a person, and she still really loves him. Once again, she is blaming herself for something she didn't do. She did not choose an evil person. She chose the good, kind, and respectful person he pretended to be when they first met. She had no idea who he really was.

It is unimaginable that the person who once treated her like a queen has turned into a monster. How could any man mistreat his partner so cruelly, whether mentally and/or physically? It doesn't make any sense to a rational person, but the abuser is *not* rational. He has little or no ability to feel empathy and can be missing a conscience. No one can reason with or predict the behavior of someone so mentally disturbed. The abused woman fell in love with the mask the abuser wore during courtship, the same mask he puts on to go out into the world each day. She keeps waiting for that kind person to return, until one day she finally realizes he *was never that person.*

Lacking an understanding of the dynamics of domestic violence: The abused woman typically lacks an understanding of the facts and consequences of domestic violence. She believes the cause of the violence is within her instead of within the abuser. She believes the problem is temporary and caused by external circumstances (like financial worries or stress at work). She believes once the stress is relieved the beatings will stop or "If I lose weight, or keep the house cleaner, or wear different clothes, he'll love me again."

Given the situation, all of these beliefs are normal, but none of them are true. An abuser will mistreat any woman. No matter what changes she makes, she does not possess the power to stop the abuse.

Believing that staying is best for the children: Many abused women believe their children need a father figure and don't want the kids to suffer from divorce. Women who stay for this reason are unaware that children suffer more long-lasting trauma from being in an abusive two-parent home than in a safe, single-parent home. She hasn't yet realized that while the fear and trauma of leaving are temporary, choosing to stay means the pain and abuse will never stop for her *or* for the children.

It's hard for any woman to look past the immediate situation when her life is consumed by survival, so it's understandable she hasn't considered how leaving provides not only relief from the immediate situation but also the potential for a healthy future relationship with a wonderful husband/father figure.

Being emotionally addicted to the abuse: This reason is listed in many books on the subject of abuse. I've also heard it mentioned on television programs dealing with the subject. Still, I had difficulty accepting that some women stay in an abusive relationship because they are addicted to the emotional highs and lows of living with an abusive partner.

None of the sources I consulted offered a suitable explanation until I came across the book *Molecules of Emotion* by Dr. Candace Pert. Dr. Pert is a research professor in the department of physiology and biophysics at Georgetown University Medical Center in Washington, DC. Her groundbreaking research led to the discovery of how the chemicals inside our body form a dynamic information network, linking mind and body. In a nutshell, her research demonstrated that our emotions have a biomolecular basis.

To give you a brief description of why we become addicted to emotions, I have to begin with Dr. Pert's initial discovery of our cellular opiate receptors (as explained here to the best of my non-scientific abilities). She determined that these receptors line some of our cell walls. The hypothalamus, a region of the brain that controls an immense number of bodily functions, produces neuropeptides (molecules that influence neural activity by carrying information directly to the cells). Certain neuropeptides are internally generated opiates. Yes, we actually possess our own internal pharmacy. Our thoughts signal the release of these powerful internal chemicals, which then bind with their corresponding opiate receptors on the walls of our cells, and our bodies feel the result.

Moreover, every external drug has an internal counterpart. In other words, pharmaceutical drugs (external drugs) are designed to mimic the neuropeptides our body produces (internal drugs) and bind to the appropriate cell receptors. That's why they work!

Repeated use of an external drug with addictive properties causes our cell receptors to crave a particular set of these pseudo-neuropeptides. This craving is what causes addiction.

So what does drug addiction have to do with emotions? Everything! Through continued research, Dr. Pert was able to confirm the connection between our emotions and our body's information network. Emotions also cause the hypothalamus to generate certain peptides, and these peptides—molecules of emotion, if you will—also bond to cell receptors. As with drug addiction, repeated "use" of the same emotion causes the receptors to crave the peptides associated with it.

Have you ever known someone you would describe as a "drama queen"? Perhaps you are witnessing that person's emotional addiction. For example, we can become addicted to the following emotions:

- Fear

- Insecurity

- Stress

- Worry

- Control

- Anger

- Inflexibility

- Self-righteousness

In an abusive situation, the continuous cycle of stimulus and response generates the same emotions again and again. For instance, the victim does or says whatever is necessary to quell the current upheaval of her abusive partner. Having once again become the savior of the relationship, her extreme fear turns to tremendous relief until he flares up again, at which point the cycle is repeated.

An emotional addiction to these extreme highs and lows clouds our judgment. In her book *Men Who Hate Women and the Women Who Love Them*, Dr. Susan Forward discusses the importance of helping her patients acknowledge and break this addiction in order to prevent them from returning to a recently severed abusive relationship. Although not all victims become emotional addicts, the addiction can be so strong that some women, even after successfully severing an abusive relationship, will return.

Chapter 18

The Making and Mindset of an Abuser

Abuse is "the systematic persecution of one partner by another.
Any behavior that is designed to control and subjugate another
human being through use of fear, humiliation
and verbal or physical assault" constitutes abuse.

—Dr. Susan Forward

The Creation of an Abusive Man

*F*amily influence: A boy does not have to be raised in an abusive environment to receive a message of male entitlement. His father or another male role model doesn't have to explicitly state that females are inferior, but when the conduct of the man of the house includes behaviors such as making all the decisions, always having the last word in an argument, encouraging the boy not to act like a girl, making fun of women's sports, voicing demeaning comments about women running for political office, and/or expecting his household and his needs to be taken care of solely by the woman of the house, the boy subliminally absorbs the message that men should be dominant and women submissive.

When the female in the household has unknowingly internalized this age-old patriarchal definition of her role in the home and her limited career opportunities in the world, she may exhibit full acceptance, even contentment, with the inequality of her situation.

The boy will grow up integrating the belittling beliefs associated with male superiority into his understanding of how things should be in the world. As a consequence, he will expect the female he chooses to cater to him at the expense of her own wants, needs, and career aspirations.

171

An abusive upbringing: A man who comes from an abusive background has strong mixed feelings toward his mother. On the one hand, she was abused. On the other, she was weak and didn't stand up to her abuser, didn't protect her child, and didn't provide the security the child so desperately needed. As children, these men found themselves in a no-win situation: wanting to save their mother and at the same time resenting her for not fighting back and for not being there for them.

If a man was put into the position as a young boy of being his abused mother's rescuer, he may feel totally overwhelmed by a woman's needs when he is an adult. His partner's legitimate expectations of emotional and/or physical support can trigger a barrage of emotions from those times in his childhood when he felt terribly inadequate. Not wanting to relive this hurt and unwilling to confront his past, the abuser reacts with disgust, anger, and/or contempt when the woman in his life expresses any kind of pain, want, need, or illness.

Whether his mother was the subject of abuse or was a domineering, over-possessive, cold matriarch, the son grows up harboring the same issues: desperation for the love he never received and extreme fear of abandonment.

Boys raised in an abusive household can grow up to hold a range of distorted beliefs:

- Control is the only way to guarantee love and devotion.

- Abusing a woman is an acceptable and effective way to control her.

- The man's way is the only way.

- Respect is not part of a relationship.

- Men are powerful and women are weak.

- Women exist solely to serve men.

- Domination and control of a woman is proof of masculinity.

Community influence: When a boy is raised in a home where his father assaults his mother but never seems to get into any serious trouble because of it, he absorbs the message that the father's behavior is considered acceptable by the community.

Mistreatment of women is rampant in some communities. Boys raised in this environment grow up to believe that abusing the women in their lives is not only a community norm, it is the way men everywhere are supposed to treat women.

Media messages: Media in our patriarchal society infuse women with the notion that their value is a function of how they are viewed by men. Women are encouraged to strive for male attention via their appearance and taught they must have a man in their life in order to have value. Men receive a very different and dangerous message.

Through TV, videos, popular songs, and pornography, men are encouraged to view women as sex objects and valueless, second-class citizens. These subliminal messages fuel men's feelings of entitlement to control, manipulate, and possess the women in their lives. For some, inequitable treatment of women at home and in the workplace becomes an accepted norm. For the man with abusive tendencies, these media messages of cruelty and partner exploitation only serve to reinforce his unbalanced life view.

Some of the more overt forms of discrimination against women have been tamed in recent decades by a combination of statute and public pressure. However, there is a whole other level of discrimination and male entitlement that is much more subtle, a level ingrained to such an extent that it often goes unnoticed by both genders.

Religion: A man's early religious upbringing can be formative in his relationships, his perception of women, and his beliefs regarding the entitlement of men. This is not surprising when you consider that women are instructed by the holy books of major religions to submit to male domination and banned by some sects from becoming spiritual leaders. The fact that some religious texts contain passages depicting women as evil and sinister further feeds the abuser's distorted way of thinking. Although more nuanced interpretations of these holy writings may be less damaging to women, the abuser will latch on to whatever interpretation supports his behavior.

Professionals who attempt to counsel abusive men report instances where men rely on quotations from religious texts to justify the abuse of their partners.

Are There Any Stable Men Out There?

After reading this chapter you may be wondering if there are any men who aren't already abusers or, at minimum, teetering on the fence. The answer to this question is a resounding YES! Even though our culture encourages men to see women as subservient (albeit sometimes unintentionally), many men consciously reject this message.

The world is full of wonderful, caring, respectful men who recognize the value, equality, and dignity of all people. In order to be strong, they do not need you to be weak. In order to feel powerful, they do not need to make you feel powerless. In order to love you, they do not have to change you, because you are whole and beautiful and strong just as you are. This is the type of partner you deserve. Never settle for anything less!

Chapter 19

Your Basic Human Relationship Rights

"The future belongs to those who believe in the beauty of their dreams."
—Eleanor Roosevelt

*E*very human being, regardless of gender, race, ethnicity, religious affiliation, or marital status, has the following basic relationship rights:

- You have the right for your needs and feelings to be held as equally important as anyone else's needs and feelings.

- You have the right to experience and express your feelings.

- You have the right to express your opinions.

- You have the right to set your own priorities.

- You have the right to establish independence.

- You have the right to decide how to spend your time.

- You have the right to choose your own lifestyle.

- You have the right to change your lifestyle, yourself, your behaviors, your values, your life situation, and your mind.

- You have the right to dress, wear your hair, and feed and maintain your body as you choose.

- You have the right to read, watch, or listen to whatever you want.

- You have the right to choose your path in this world and the type of work you prefer.

- You have the right to make honest mistakes and to admit those mistakes without being humiliated.

- You have the right to self-fulfillment through your own talents and interests.

- You have the right to grow as a person and to accept new challenges.

- You have the right to choose with whom you spend your time and with whom you share your body.

- You have the right to be treated with dignity and respect in all your relationships.

- You have the right to be listened to respectfully.

- You have the right to ask for what you want assertively.

- You have the right to say "I don't understand" or "I don't know" without being humiliated.

- You have the right to say "No" and to set limits and boundaries without feeling guilty. (Each of us has the right to ask for what we want of another person, as well as the right to say no to another's request.)

- You have the right to set limits on how you will be treated in your relationships.

- You have the right to expect your boundaries to be respected.

- You have the right to walk away from toxic or abusive relationships.

- You have the right to pursue what makes you happy.

- You have the right to stand up for yourself and to demand that your rights be respected.

Healthy personal boundaries are based on this foundation of basic rights, and no group or organization, society, religion, culture, or individual has the right to take any of them from you.

Good relationships are based on trust, integrity, mutual respect, and honoring these basic rights to which all human beings are entitled. Unfortunately, in our patriarchal society, the majority of men ignore these boundaries to one degree or another when it comes to women. This long-standing norm has become so deeply ingrained in our culture that it frequently goes unnoticed, causing it to be unwittingly supported by both genders. As long as male entitlement and domination rule, abuse of women will continue.

By knowing your basic human rights and refusing to let anyone invade your personal space without your permission, you are caring for yourself and teaching any man who wishes to be part of your life that he must respect you or move on. Men must learn to recognize and honor the line where they end and you begin. The more often women refuse to allow men to disregard their boundaries, the faster our society will begin to change. By taking this stand we are also deterring male dominance from being passed down to future generations.

Exposing the Role of Entitlement in Abusive Relationships

In an article titled "Let's End Relationship Entitlement Now," Thomas G. Fiffer, MA, senior editor, ethics, at The Good Men Project, presents a five-point manifesto that illustrates the role of entitlement in abusive relationships [*italics added for emphasis*].[23]

1. **Our relationship does not entitle you to have sex with me.** Not every night. Not every week. Not even once. Not ever. I may be your wife, husband, girlfriend, or boyfriend, but I don't have to put out. A relationship creates the opportunity for sex but does not guarantee it. Your needs are important, but they don't ever

determine the outcome. If you're not getting enough, you can leave. *Sex is requested, negotiated, and agreed on, and my consent— expressed in words or with clear, non-verbal communication—is always required.* [To this excellent list I would add one more point: *I am not responsible for your orgasm!*]

2. **Our relationship does not entitle you to treat me with disrespect.** There is nothing I can do to you that merits contempt or scorn. You may be upset with me, disappointed, even angry, and you have every right to express these feelings in a healthy, constructive way. But you have no right to insult, mock, demean, or dismiss me, or to treat me as anything but an equal. *I don't stick around where I'm not appreciated.*

3. **Our relationship does not entitle you to use physical force against me, except in self-defense.** If I start beating you up, you have every right to defend yourself and subdue me. Otherwise, you must never strike me, push me, restrain me, or interfere with my physical freedom. You must respect my body space at all times. No matter how angry you are—with me or anything else in your life—and no matter how much you may hurt inside, hurting me physically is never an option. If a stranger attacked me, I would call the police, and *our relationship will not prevent me from calling them on you.*

4. **Our relationship does not entitle you to emotional manipulation,** to use my fears and vulnerabilities to hurt me or get your needs met. If I don't want to do something, I don't want to do it, and I get to choose not to do it. If you want to convince me otherwise, give me a good reason. Show me the benefit for me. If you threaten pain for non-compliance, I will lose all respect for you, instantly. *And I will pack my bags (if I live with you) and leave.*

5. **Our relationship does not entitle you to assume you're fine and leave your own issues, illnesses, and disorders untreated.** Just because I'm dating you, or married to you, I don't have to accept your hurtful behavior and destructive patterns as givens.

You may have hidden these things during courtship. Or I may have ignored all your red flags. Either way, I don't have to be stuck tolerating stuff in our relationship just because we're in a relationship. *Nothing is permanent, and if you take me or my love for you for granted, you'll soon find yourself alone.*

These examples from The Good Men Project illustrate how abusers use a combination of entitlement, dominance, and privilege as a green light to treat their partners more like slaves than fellow humans with free agency. Instances of male entitlement, however, are by no means limited to abusers. They also rear their ugly head in subtle, everyday ways that need to be brought to the attention of both men and women.

Everyday Examples of Male Entitlement/Dominance/ Privilege

Elizabeth Cady Stanton, an early crusader for women's suffrage, said this in the mid-1800s: "Our religion, laws, customs, are all founded on the belief that woman was made for man." Contemporary laws, as well as most religious traditions, no longer support this premise. Nevertheless, because the *custom* of male entitlement has become engrained in our culture over the centuries, it can be common for both genders to unconsciously allow this mindset to form the framework of their relationships and their lives.

Most men do not become aware of entitlement on their own; it's often their partners who bring it to their attention. Good men will want to understand this dynamic and do their best to eliminate entitled behavior. A man who doesn't care is not worth your time.

Here are just a few examples of male entitlement you should watch for when getting to know a potential partner. (Of course, a couple can choose to relax boundaries to whatever degree they wish as they get to know one another, but if you experience these forms of entitlement right off the bat, *beware!*)

Grabs something out of your hand: In this example, a man you are just getting to know decides you are not operating the TV remote to his liking, or he simply wants to watch something different. He takes the remote out of your hand and uses it as he wants. In extreme cases, he switches channels without any regard for you. He could have said, "Would you mind if I give the remote a try?" and/or "Could we find something else to watch?"

Similarly, you are about to pour a glass of almond milk. He grabs the carton out of your hand because he thinks it should be shaken. He could have said, "Would you mind if I give the milk a shake?"

In both these cases, he has crossed the line between where he ends and you begin. He's more than disregarding your feelings and preferences. He's so focused on his own feelings (the only feelings he's been programmed to worry about) that he's unaware of the fact you might find his behavior objectionable.

On one occasion a man and I were watching a TV show at my house. As I was operating my remote, he told me what buttons to push. Why? Who knows? So, when he took the remote out of my hand, I proceeded to do the same thing to him. He made it quite clear that he was appalled by my instructions. A perfect example of how men can be totally oblivious to male entitlement, their double standards, and their belief in the ineptness of women.

Operates anything on your car while you are driving: He decides the windshield wipers are no longer needed, so he reaches across from the passenger side and turns them off. I've reminded men who are interested in eliminating entitled behavior to remember that old saying, "What's good for the goose is fine for the gander." In other words, would they ever reach over and operate the wipers on the car while their significant other is driving, if it meant she was free to do the same to them?

Provides unsolicited advice or criticism: Let's say you have invited a man to dinner. This is the first time he will be in your home. As you're cooking, he tells you what he thinks are better ways to prepare the meal. He feels free to open your fridge and pantry and criticize your food preferences. He stands next to you while you're doing dishes and tells you when you haven't cleaned an item to his liking.

He might comment on how he likes your hair better when you wear it a different way or says you would look better in different clothing.

None of this behavior is acceptable. You did not ask for his opinion in any of these instances. In each example he physically or verbally crossed into your personal space, ignoring your boundaries and rights by feeling entitled to give you his unsolicited opinion, and/ or to criticize your appearance or behavior. This man is not worth your time. His conduct has gone beyond male entitlement and indicates control issues.

A good man would offer to help you prepare the meal while taking your instructions on how to do what was necessary. He also would help you do the dishes or volunteer to do them for you. He would never feel he has the right to critique your appearance or dietary preferences. The guy in the above example is not partner material.

Feels entitled to your talents and possessions: He doesn't have a washer or dryer, so he feels entitled to bring his laundry to your house without asking. Because you can sew, he brings any of his clothing to you that needs to be altered or repaired and simply expects you to take care of it – no need to ask. Both of these examples are not only indications of male entitlement and *rude*, they are giant red flags.

181

If he asked permission to bring his laundry or sewing, would it still be an example of male entitlement? Assuming you barely know each other, the answer is YES. Asking for favors very early in a relationship not only shows he's clueless regarding male privilege, it can indicate his belief that women exist as domestic slaves. He may be looking for a mommy to whom he can offload as much of life's tedium as possible. Move on.

Believes his needs are more important than yours: When a man says no, it means no. In our society, however, most men are encouraged to believe their needs come first, so when a woman says no they unwittingly believe they have the right to ignore her preferences and do their best to change her mind. This situation plays out again and again in movies and on TV shows. As soon as a woman says no to a request from a man, indicating she has other plans or work responsibilities, the man does his best to convince her to put her own needs on the back burner and comply with his wishes. If doing what he wants compromises her work or her personal life, so what? And the script has her giving in, over and over again.

Once you're aware of this form of entitlement, it becomes easier to stand your ground and explain to the man that although he most likely doesn't mean to, he's not hearing you, he's disrespecting your wishes, and he needs to remember when you say no, *it means no*. If he continues to push to get his way, it means he's either unwilling or unable to hear you. Show him the door.

These are just a few of the ways in which male entitlement can manifest itself. Sadly, most of us have become so programmed we can fail to recognize when we're on the receiving end. If you're feeling uncomfortable about an interaction with a potential partner but not sure if you've been the recipient of male entitlement, ask yourself the following question: How would your partner feel if you did the same thing to him? If he wouldn't be happy about it, you have your answer.

❦

There are many good men who want to understand male entitlement and, when indicated, change their behavior. For this to happen, however, both genders need to become educated on the subject so they can work together to support and respect each other.

I highly recommend watching the documentaries *Miss Representation* and *The Mask You Live In*. These excellent films address the damaging messages both genders unconsciously absorb from the media and other sources. Google *The Representation Project* to watch the trailers and/or purchase these films. Google www.justwatch.com to find out where they are currently streaming.

Chapter 20

How to Investigate a Potential Partner

"It isn't what we don't know that gives us trouble,
It's what we know that ain't so."

—Will Rogers

*O*ne of the best ways to check out a potential partner is through the Internet. Even a fairly simple search can reveal a huge amount of information, including the man's full name, criminal record, arrests, relatives, financial info (bankruptcy), age, history of home ownership, current and previous addresses, participation in social media, and more. To conduct such a search, you'll need his first and last name and the city/state where he lives. If he refuses to give you this information, he's obviously trying to hide something. He might be married, in a relationship, operating a fake dating site, or living somewhere other than the location listed in his dating profile. *Time to stop all communication.*

A seemingly kind man may make you question the necessity of a background check, but I encourage you to look him up anyway. Abusers and criminals can be extremely talented con artists; in fact, it could be said that the nicer the man, the more important the investigation. Think of the serial rapists and murderers who appeared to be kind, upstanding citizens before they were caught.

It's also important to remember that what he does for a living has no bearing on the likelihood of his being or not being an abuser or otherwise unsuitable partner. For example, I turned down multiple dating invitations from a man who is an assistant minister at a local church. In addition to not being a match, my gut told me something just wasn't right. I made it quite clear I didn't want to date him, but he continued to pursue me, disrespecting my wishes. He kept trying to convince me to travel with him to dances in neighboring cities. There were plenty of dances in our area. No way was I going to get into this man's car. I didn't even know him. When he could no longer pretend to ignore my lack of interest and realized he was not going to get his way, he became quite nasty. Had I not trusted my gut, I shudder to think what might have happened.

Background-checking sites: Background-checking sites like BeenVerified, Truthfinder, InstantCheckMate, and PeopleLooker are not free, but they cost far less than a private investigator, and the investment is well worth it. If it turns out your potential date is a model citizen, you've just bought yourself peace of mind. If anything questionable surfaces, you'll have the tools to address it. Either way, who knows what you'll discover?

At the time of this writing, the cost of a report from one of these sites ranges from $18 to $34 and may include the ability to run an unlimited number of additional checks for one month. Some sites offer monthly memberships only, as opposed to charging for a single report. If you choose one of these, be sure to cancel before the second month rolls around to avoid ongoing fees.

Courthouse records: Unfortunately, marital status and injunctions (restraining orders/protective orders) are not part of background-site reports, due to the inability of these sites to access public court records. If a man claims he was divorced in Ohio, for example, begin your search by Googling *how to find divorce records in Ohio*. You'll normally need his full name and the county where the divorce took place. Some states offer online access. If the state or county website does not provide divorce records, phone the appropriate courthouse directly. They will look up the information for you. Information on how to access court records by state can also be found by Googling *How to Look Up Court Records On the Internet - Links to Online Access to Records in Other States*. Scroll down to see a list by state.

Phone-number searches: Google *whitepages* to discover a phonebook-like site that offers a premium service for about $5 a month, although some information is available at no charge. You can search by phone number, name/location, or a specific address. Depending upon which one you choose, you may receive free information regarding name, city/state, age range, address, and/or a list of potential relatives/associates. The information may not be 100 percent accurate. When I put in my name and location, it showed I had once lived in Virginia Beach, which is not true, but the rest of the information was correct.

Google picture search: A picture search can also reveal information about the man you're thinking about meeting. The process is simple. Right click on his dating-site picture and "save as" to your computer. Then go to images.google.com. You'll see a small camera icon in the Google search window. If you click on the camera icon and follow the prompts to upload the photo, Google will return a list of other locations on the web where the picture can be found. These additional locations may provide revealing information.

I once used this type of search to reveal details about a man pictured in a military uniform and, guess what, his profile was fake. The page Google images found provided details about the man in addition to his picture. Among other facts that didn't match, he was actually ten years younger than the age stated in the fake dating profile. Needless to say, the fake profile was reported and removed. *Be thorough to be safe!*

We are the authors of our lives.
We write our own daring endings.
We craft love from heartbreak,
compassion from shame,
grace from disappointment,
and courage from failure.
Showing up is our power.
Story is our way home. Truth is our song.
We are the brave and brokenhearted.
We are rising strong.

—excerpt from the poem "Manifesto of the Brave and Brokenhearted"
By Nayyirah Waheed[24]

⊜⊷⊱⊰⊹⊰⊱⊶⊜

Thank you for choosing this book. I hope it has opened the door to your freedom, your healing, and your new life. May that life be overflowing with love, support, kindness, joy, and lots of laughter.

From my heart to yours,
T. Ann DeCarlo

Chapter 21

Resources and References

Hotline Telephone Numbers

- National Domestic Violence Hotline: 1-800-799-SAFE (7233)

- National Sexual Assault Hotline: 1-800-656-HOPE (4673)

- National Child Abuse Hotline: 1-800-4-A-CHILD (422-4453)

- National Suicide Prevention Lifeline: 988 OR 1-800-273-TALK (8255)

- Victim Information & Notification Everyday (VINE): 1-866-277-7477

Books

Brown, Sandra L., MA, *How to Spot a Dangerous Man Before You Get Involved.* Alameda, CA: Hunter House Inc., 2005.

> Sandra L. Brown holds a master's degree in counseling, with a specialty in personality disorders/pathology. She is CEO of The Institute for Relational Harm Reduction & Public Pathology Education, as well as a program development specialist, lecturer, community educator, and award-winning author.

Forward, Susan, PhD, and Joan Torres. *Men Who Hate Women and the Women Who Love Them.* New York: Bantam Books, 1987.

Susan Forward is one of the nation's leading therapists, as well as a bestselling author, dynamic lecturer, and frequent talk-show guest. In addition to her private practice, she has served as a therapist, instructor, and consultant for many Southern California psychiatric and medical facilities. She also hosted her own nationally syndicated program on ABC Talk Radio for six years.

Hamburg, Sam R., PhD, *Will Our Love Last*. New York: Scribner, 2001.

Sam Hamburg is a clinical psychologist and marital therapist in private practice, a lecturer in the Department of Psychiatry at the University of Chicago's Pritzker School of Medicine, and a member of the adjunct faculty of The Family Institute at Northwestern University. He lives in Chicago, Illinois. *Will Our Love Last* is a best-selling step-by-step guide to choosing a life partner based on sexual, practical, and emotional compatibility.

Norwood, Robin. Women *Who Love Too Much*. New York: Pocket Books, 1985, 1997, and 2008.

Robin Norwood is a former marriage, family, and child therapist specializing in the treatment of chemical dependency and codependency.

Pert, Candace. PhD. *Molecules of Emotion*. New York: Scribner, 2010.

Candace Pert (1946–2013), was an internationally recognized neuroscientist and pharmacologist who published over 250 research articles. She was featured in Bill Moyers' book (and subsequent PBS documentary) *Healing and the Mind*, in the PBS show *Healing Quest*, and in the book *Happy for No Reason* by Marci Shimoff. In the 1980s, Dr. Pert was a significant contributor to the emergence of mind-body medicine as an area of legitimate scientific research, earning her the titles of "The Mother of Psychoneuroimmunology," and "The Goddess of Neuroscience" from her many fans.

Abuse Awareness and Educational Groups

Domestic Shelters: DomesticShelters.org, A Service of Theresa's Fund; *Domesticshelters.org* online; www.domesticshelters.org/help#?page=1

Theresa's Fund is an Arizona-based charity started in 1992 to change the landscape of domestic violence in the state. In 2014, the fund developed DomesticShelters.org to expand its services throughout the United States and Canada. To find shelters in your area, enter your zip code or the name of your city in the search box displayed.

Live Your Dream: Soroptimist; *Live Your Dream* online; "Get Help/Domestic Violence Resources"; https://www.liveyourdream.org/get-help/apply-for-an-educational-grant/index.html

Soroptimist is a service organization founded by women for women. Through more than 1,300 clubs in twenty-one countries and territories, it provides resources, education, and grants for victims of domestic violence. Educational grants are awarded each year to over 1,700 women.

The application period opens on August 1 each year and remains open until November 15. There are nine requirements for eligibility. The two most important are: (1) You must be the primary source of financial support for your family; and (2) You must be enrolled in or have been accepted to a vocational/skills training program or an undergraduate degree program. The link listed above leads to a page where you can view a complete list of requirements and begin the application process.

The "Domestic Violence Resources" option under the Get Help tab provides additional information on resources related to domestic abuse, as well as a video on how to seek a protective order (restraining order/injunction) against an abusive partner. Although not mentioned in the video, it's important to remember that many domestic violence shelters offer assistance with preparing and filing protective orders.

Love is Respect: National Domestic Violence Hotline; *Love is Respect* online; www.loveisrespect.org/about/ (phone 1-866-331-9474); text (text LOVEIS to 22522). A live chat feature is also available on the site.

Love is Respect offers free and confidential information, support, and advocacy, 24/7, to young people between the ages of thirteen and twenty-six who have questions or concerns about their romantic relationships. Free support is also available to concerned friends and family members, teachers, counselors, and other service providers.

Headings on the site include "About Dating, Healthy Relationships, Personal Safety, and Supporting Others" and offer tips to prevent unhealthy relationships or disrupt ongoing relationships that are or are likely to become harmful.

Mosaic: Gavin de Becker & Associates; *Mosaic Threat Assessment Systems* online; "Domestic Violence/Male Offender Questionnaire"; www.mosaicmethod.com

Gavin de Becker is an expert in the prediction and prevention of violence. This questionnaire is designed to assess your level of danger. It works by breaking a situation down into its elements, factor-by-factor, and then seeing what picture emerges when the pieces of the puzzle are put together. The Mosaic questionnaire helps an assessor weigh a current situation in light of expert opinion and research and compare it rapidly with past cases where the outcomes are known.

National Domestic Violence Hotline: website of the National Domestic Violence Hotline; *National Domestic Violence Hotline* online; www.thehotline.org/help/

Clicking on the referenced link offers three ways to access the hotline immediately: the 800 number, a number to text, and a button that opens a chat window, which for some women may be a safer alternative than a phone or text. In addition, clicking on any of the options across the top of the page provides information on a variety of topics related to abuse, available resources, etc.

Safe Havens for Pets: a service of the Animal Welfare Institute (AWI); www.safehavensforpets.org

In 2011 AWI established the Safe Havens Mapping Project to provide an inclusive list of sheltering services for animals, accessible to individuals experiencing domestic violence. The site is updated on a regular basis to provide accurate, up-to-date information. Depending on the area, services range from dedicated kennel space at humane societies to foster care homes to domestic violence shelters that maintain or partner with pet care facilities. Accessing this site brings up a page with a spot to enter a zip code or the name of a city to find a nearby place to house your animals safely.

VINE: Victim Information & Notification Everyday; www.vinelink.com/#state-selection

Established in 1994, this service allows crime victims and other concerned citizens to learn the status of a perpetrator's incarceration. For more information, access the VINE website or call customer service at 1-866-277-7477.

WomensLaw: National Network to End Domestic Violence (NNEDV); *WomensLaw.org* online; www.womenslaw.org

This site provides legal information in plain language for victims of abuse. To find out about the laws in your area, click on the search window (hourglass) in the upper right corner of the site, then click on the Go button. When the search screen appears, enter the name of your state.

Stalking, Cyberstalking, and Technology Safety

Action Against Stalking: the website of Action Against Stalking; *Action Against Stalking* online; www.actionagainststalking.org

This organization was founded in 2014 by Ann Moulds, who was a victim of stalking in her home country of Scotland.

Cyber Civil Rights: the website of Cyber Civil Rights Initiative (CCRI); *Cyber Civil Rights Initiative* online; www.cybercivilrights.org (Helpline 1-844-878-2274).

CCRI works to combat online abuses that threaten civil rights and civil liberties. Their research indicates that one in eight adult social media users has been the target of nonconsensual pornography. CCRI can offer help to these and other victims of image-based sexual abuse, including the potential to intervene in legal cases in a victim's defense.

The Victim Services option under the "What We Do" tab at the top of the site offers an Online Image Removal Guide as well as the ability to view laws for each state regarding nonconsensual pornography, sextortion, and deep fakes (the manipulation of visual and audio images/sounds with the intention to deceive).

Cyberstalking: *Fight Cyberstalking* online; www.fightcyberstalk ing.org

This organization was started by Lisa Woeller, who was harassed by a cyberstalker in the U.S. from 2006 to 2018. Download her free *Fight Cyberstalking Toolkit.*

Technology Assistance: Geek Squad Services at Best Buy.

It's worth asking these technicians if they can help you with stalking issues that involve your electronic devices. Maybe they can tell if there is a tracking app on your phone. Your phone service provider might also be helpful.

Technology Safety: the website of the National Network to End Domestic Violence; *Technology Safety*; www.techsafety.org

This site contains important information related to the impact of technology on intimate partner violence, sexual assault, and violence against women. The Survivor Toolkit, listed in the dropdown menu under the Resources tab at the top of the page, covers relevant topics such as a Technology Safety Plan, Documenting Abuse, a Survivors' Guide to Phones, and Online Privacy & Safety.

Helping Someone Who is Experiencing Abuse

Supporting Others: the website of the National Domestic Violence Hotline; *The Hotline* online; "Support Others"; www.thehotline.org/support-others/ways-to-support-a-domestic-violence-survivor/

Those with a friend or loved one who is involved in an abusive relationship or who has recently left such a relationship and is trying to put her life back together may find this reference helpful.

Additional Recommendations

In addition to the resources listed above, you may want to consider the following:

Brown, Brené, PhD. The Gifts of Imperfection: *Let Go of Who You Think You're Supposed to Be and Embrace Who You Are.* Center City, MN: Hazelden Publishing, 2010.

> Brené Brown is a research professor at the University of Houston where she holds the Huffington Foundation Chair endowed in her name at the Graduate College of Social Work. Dr. Brown has spent the past two decades studying courage, vulnerability, shame, and empathy and is the author of five #1 *New York Times* bestsellers: *The Gifts of Imperfection, Daring Greatly, Rising Strong, Braving the Wilderness,* and her latest book, *Dare to Lead,* which is the culmination of a seven-year study on courage and leadership.

Gilbert, Elizabeth. *Committed: A Love Story.* New York: Riverhead Books, 2009.

> At the end of her best-selling memoir *Eat, Pray, Love,* Elizabeth Gilbert writes of falling in love with Felipe, a Brazilian living in Indonesia. The couple swears eternal love but also (as skittish divorce survivors) swears never to marry. Providence intervened in the form of a U.S. government ultimatum: marry or Felipe can never enter America again.

> Having been effectively sentenced to wed, Gilbert tackles her fears by delving into the history and practices of the stubbornly enduring institution of marriage. *Committed* records her journey to define the essence of marriage through historical research, interviews, and personal reflection. Told with her trademark wit, intelligence, and compassion, Gilbert attempts to "turn on all the lights" when it comes to matrimony: compatibility,

infatuation, fidelity, family traditions, social expectations, divorce risks, and humbling responsibilities. The result is a clear-eyed celebration of love with all of the complexity and consequence that real love, in the real world, entails.

The Good Men Project: the website of The Good Men Project; *The Good Men Project*; www.goodmenproject.com/

> The Good Men Project, founded by Tom Matlack in 2009, provides a forum for, as described on the website, "a much-needed cultural conversation about manhood."

Gottman, John Mordecai, PhD. *Why Marriages Succeed or Fail: And How You Can Make Yours Last.* New York: Simon & Schuster, 1995.

> John Gottman, professor emeritus of psychology at the University of Washington, is a psychologist who has spent decades studying what makes marriages work. He has earned numerous awards for his research on marriage and parenting and is the author or coauthor of forty books.

Psychology Today: the website of *Psychology Today. Psychology Today* online; www.psychologytoday.com/us

You can learn more about personality disorders by searching this site for the name of the disorder.

Stout, Martha, PhD. *The Sociopath Next Door.* New York: Harmony Books, 2006.

Martha Stout is a clinical psychologist who served on the faculty in the department of psychiatry at Harvard Medical School for twenty-five years. Her book provides an in-depth look at sociopathy and how to recognize it in those around us.

Notes

1   Mary Oliver, "The Journey," first published in *No Voyage and Other Poems*, Stowmarket, United Kingdom: Dent Press, 1963. Used with permission from Grove Atlantic.

2   Different states may use one or more of these terms and, depending upon the circumstances, these terms may represent different legal initiatives or parameters.

3   A condom is not 100 percent effective, especially when dealing with chlamydia or human papillomavirus (HPV). And some forms of HPV can cause genital warts or cancer. Because each of these diseases is transmitted by simple skin-to-skin contact and can be asymptomatic, it's a very good idea to insist that a sexually active potential partner be tested for both. You may also want to be tested if you have been sexually active or if your abuser was not faithful. Testing for HPV is now a standard component of an annual female exam.

4   Emotional abuse is also known as psychological or mental abuse.

5   Malathi L. Perugula, Puneet D. Narang, Steven B. Lippman, https://doi/10.4088/PCC.16br02076, The Primary Care Companion for CNS Disorders, "The Biological Basis to Personality Disorders," Physicians Postgraduate Press, Inc. (2017).

6   Tina de Benedictis, PhD, Jaelline Jaffe, PhD, Jeanne Segal, PhD, www.helpguide.org, "Domestic Violence and Abuse: Types, Signs, Symptoms, Causes, and Effects," American Academy of Experts in Traumatic Stress (AAETS), www.aaets.org/traumatic-stress-library/domestic-violence-and-abuse-types-signs-symptoms-causes-and-effects (last accessed April 2022).

7   Ibid.

8   George Simon, PhD, "The Possessive Thinking of the Disturbed Character," www.drgeorgesimon.com/the-possessive-thinking-of-the-disturbed-character/ (last accessed April 2022)

9   George Simon, PhD, "Severe Character Disorders," www.drgeorgesimon.com/severe-character-disorders/ (last accessed April 2022).

10 The National Domestic Violence Hotline, "Should I Go To Couples Therapy with My Abusive Partner?" www.thehotline.org/resources/should-i-go-to-couples-therapy-with-my-abusive-partner/ (last accessed April 2022).

11 You can get information from the VINE website at www.vinelink.com, or contact customer service at 1-866-277-7477. The customer service line is staffed 24 hours a day, 365 days a year.

12 Soroptimist is a service organization founded by women for women. Through more than 1,300 clubs in twenty-one countries and territories, the organization provides education and training assistance to women and girls. Since 1972, more than 30,000 women have been helped by the Live Your Dream awards. Today more than half of each year's award recipients are survivors of domestic violence, trafficking, or sexual assault.

13 The information in this chapter is based on the services and programs available at a domestic violence center in my area. Specific names for or composition of programs may vary from state to state. The range and structure of organizations providing different services will also vary from state to state and area to area.

14 Robin Norwood, *Women Who Love Too Much*, New York: Pocket Books (1985, 1997, and 2008).

15 Hot in Cleveland was an original series than ran on the TV Land channel from 2010 to 2015.

16 At the time of this writing, *Misrepresentation* is available for purchase on streaming sites such as iTunes and Vimeo on Demand. You can also purchase the DVD and/or watch the trailer by Googling The Representation Project.

17 Like Miss Representation, the documentary *The Mask You Live In* was also written and produced by Jennifer Siebel Newsom. Also available for purchase on DVD, it addresses how society's definition of masculinity is harming boys.

18 Leon F. Seltzer, PhD., "The 'I Feel Like a Child' Syndrome," Psychology Today website, posted December 24, 2008. You can read the entire article by Googling it.

19 Ibid.

20 Ibid.

21 Ibid.

22 Matthew Arnold, "Self-Dependence," adaptation of lines 31–32, *Poetical Works of Matthew Arnold*. London: MacMillan and Co., 1895.

23 Thomas G. Fiffer, MA, "Let's End Relationship Entitlement Now," written for The Good Men Project. https://goodmenproject.com/ethics-values/lets-end-relationship-entitlement-fiff/ (last accessed April 2022).

24 Brené Brown, PhD, *Rising Strong: How the Ability to Reset Transforms the Way We Live, Love, Parent and Lead*, New York: Random House (2017). The title of this book was inspired by the poem "Manifesto of the Brave and Brokenhearted" by Nayyirah Waheed, which appears on www.brenebrown.com. Used with permission from a representative of Brené Brown.

Made in the USA
Coppell, TX
22 May 2023

17162879R00129